Artwork by Robert Hopey

OBLIVION

For Roger
Bless your ministry with
our Brothers & Sisters on the
streets.

Live Love!

[signature] 2019

OBLIVION

Grace in Exile With a Monk Behind Bars

By **Dennis Gibbs**

ob·liv·i·on

noun

- the state of being completely forgotten or unknown
- the state of being unconscious or unaware
- the state of being destroyed

ISBN: 9781798765661

Front cover design by Carrie Voris
Book design by Janet Kawamoto
Editors: Lizze Slocum, Alysha Kawamoto

Printed by Cathedral Center Press
in the United States of America.

First printing edition 2019

Cathedral Center Press
840 Echo Park Avenue
Los Angeles, California 90026
editor@ladiocese.org

Proceeds from sales of *Oblivion* benefit
the work of PRISM Restorative Justice,
a ministry of the Episcopal Diocese of Los Angeles.
www.prismjustice.org

For Evelyn

You suffered too long at the brutal hands
of domestic violence and died too young from the
ravages of alcoholism. May you now rest eternally
in the gentle, loving arms of God.

Contents

Foreword   ix

Chapter One: The Invitation   1

Chapter Two: Exile   9

Chapter Three: Idaho   17

Chapter Four: Movin' On   47

Chapter Five: Oblivion   77

Chapter Six: New Year's Eve   91

Chapter Seven: The Narrow Gate   99

Chapter Eight: Holy • Holy • Holy   127

Chapter Nine: Seeing   157

Chapter Ten: Returning   163

Gratitude   174

Foreword

How did Jesus heal? Sometimes he did it with a word and a command. Often he would touch. He felt quite free to touch the leper before he even got around to healing him, which both horrified and wowed the crowd.

But with the deaf man who also couldn't speak, Jesus breaks all sorts of purity codes to arrive at healing. He puts his fingers in the guy's ears, he spits and touches his tongue (this quite scandalized the gathered). Then he looks up to heaven and he sighs greatly, and says: "Ephphatha. Be opened." Actually, the Greek word is more than "to open." It means to open in order to make a connection. I suppose, on one hand, Jesus wants the man's ears and tongue to be loosed so he can hear and speak. But perhaps he is also, in this healing, wanting the heavens to open up to us ... here and now. And wanting us to connect to each other ... here and now.

In the end, the healings are never about cure. I suppose Jesus thinks life would be better for this guy if he could hear and speak. But the healings are always about inclusion. This guy was outside and not pitied for his disability. He didn't belong nor was he welcome inside. The man was scorned and Jesus chooses to touch what ought not to be touched. And be sure not to tell anybody because they will kill me for this.

A homegirl, Sharnise, a trainee at Homeboy Industries, stands in front of a packed church in Philadelphia and tells her story. A gang member and felon, she recounts for the audience her struggle that leads her eventually to walk through the doors of our gang intervention program. She wants to say that Homeboy Industries welcomed her with open arms, but what she ends up saying is, "Homeboy opened me … with welcomed arms."

Dennis Gibbs' fine book, *Oblivion*, opened me with welcomed arms. Indeed, the "heavens" seemed to be made available in the here and now because of his testimony. Indeed, it opened me to make a connection.

There is an enduring truth throughout this account. What longs to be opened up to us is our unshakable goodness. So much blocks and impedes the hearing of it, the seeing of it and ultimately, our speaking of it … until the word ephphatha is uttered. And the healing is not just a return to speech, or to hearing for the first time … but rather, we are opened for something. The freedom to speak and hear is an opening that leads to purposeful presence and the exquisite mutuality that is God's dream come true.

I consider it one of my singular privileges on this earth to know Dennis Gibbs. The spiritual journey he recounts here, filled with unspeakable travails and endless "up-against" moments, all lead to the heavens opening up. It has been my honor to walk through the jails with Dennis and observe his humble touch and ready reception of men whose journeys greatly resemble his in hardship, terror and abject abandonment. Dennis never muddies the water with his own story to these men, but rather allows his being to receive who they are and they are opened, with welcomed arms. Dennis allows himself to be reached by these men and it ignites a healing power in them that both ennobles and heightens their dignity. They are brought inside, no longer banished beyond the edges of our compassion. It is unmistakable and remarkable to behold. As they say, perhaps those he accompanies will not remember Dennis' exact words to them, but they will never forget how he made them feel.

Unless we welcome our wounds, we will feel tempted to despise the wounded. Dennis excavates his brokenness in these pages and it leads to a cherishing that is tender and compelling. It is never about Dennis. It is about our own inhabiting of our goodness and nobility. As a great many Buddhist texts begin: "Oh nobly born … remember who you really are." The journey is not a return to the garden as a "good person" having been tossed out previously as a bad one. Rather, this journey is a recognition of our goodness, our "Buddha nature" and a solid remembering of who we really are.

Dennis Gibbs, with this telling, points beyond himself, to the God who loves us without measure and without regret. He signals, not the accomplishment of triumph over adversity, but rather the tender glance of God that beholds and sustains us. Indeed, the heavens are opened. Go ahead, sigh greatly. We aren't just restored to something new in our personal healing, but given access to something quite large and expansive. Heaven comes then in resting in the stillness of love and loving in the stillness of God.

To walk with Dennis in this sacred journey (as to accompany him in the County Jail) is to recognize a profound hospitality, an opening with welcomed arms, to the extravagance of tenderness. It compels us to look heavenward and be readied for some new, spacious connection. It propels us to be in the world who God is. It hopes for us to embrace, in his words – our sacred self, and realize everything God intends for us.

The Rev. Gregory Boyle
Founder, Homeboy Industries
Los Angeles, California
December 2018

CHAPTER ONE

The Invitation

As he walked by the Sea of Galilee, he saw two brothers, Simon, who is called Peter, and Andrew his brother, casting a net into the lake—for they were fishermen. And he said to them, 'Follow me, and I will make you fish for people.' Immediately they left their nets and followed him.

—Matthew 4:18–20

I wasn't always a monk, living in a monastery and praying four times a day. Far from it; in fact, one might even say that I started in the opposite direction. I grew up in a household that was at best agnostic toward the idea of God – at its worst, it was a place where some horrible things happened as a result of a family system saturated in alcoholism and all of the behavior associated with it. I took my own first drink as a teenager and quickly turned to pot, speed and LSD. I discovered cocaine in my mid-twenties, and from that point on, addiction ruled my life. It cost me almost everything: the promise of an exciting career, two marriages, friendships and relationships with my family, all washed down the drain by booze and dope. Addiction took me in and out of numerous jails, landed me a brief stay in a mental facility after a very real attempt to take my own life, reduced me to a life on the streets, and eventually drove me to the brink of insanity and death.

I was forty-three years old when, by God's grace, I was able to make the big turn and find recovery. I was stumbling around Los Angeles with a pocketful of cigarette butts, stealing booze and food out of supermarkets (in that order, mind you, because I had my priorities) and, as strange as it sounds, carrying a briefcase. Because after all, I was a big shot! The briefcase I clung to contained the fragments of a life that at one time held promise. There were headshots and a news article from my days as an actor, along with family keepsakes and mementos. There was a card from my sister in Idaho, mailed to me long before I went underground. My baptismal certificate from St. Frances of Assisi Church in Sacramento was there, preserved in plastic. There was the small pocket where I sometimes kept cocaine.

Clearly, I was not in my right mind. I was physically, mentally, and spiritually sick from decades of drug use; lost and dying, carrying the wounds and unreconciled heartache from trauma that had begun so long ago. I didn't know how long it had been since I had had a shower other than bird-baths in gas station bathrooms. I still remember the musky, oily odor of that life.

I know what it's like to be clinging with feeble fingers to small shreds of dignity and self-respect. For years, I lived with a sense of disbelief that I had let my life get to this point, as though it were a bad dream. But this nightmare of a life was very real, as was the deep shame that came with it. I was a pitiful mess with sunken, desperate eyes and a flagging spirit when I stumbled into a recovery meeting one New Year's Eve and begged for help.

Over the following two decades, the grace of God pulled me from back from oblivion and set me on a path of recovery that has truly revolutionized my life and my relation with God, with myself and with my brothers and sisters in the world. From an outsider's view, it may seem unlikely that a guy like me would become a monk, dedicated to walking with our incarcerated brothers and sisters in the same places that held me prisoner. But that is the life I live now, and it makes more and more sense as the years go by.

I often say that I have the best job in the world, although it's more than just a job; it's a true vocation. I didn't always feel that way; the thought of walking back into the jails, even as a free man, struck me with fear and trembling. My experiences being locked up, and the alcohol and drug-addicted life that led me there, are nothing I would wish to live through again.

My invitation to return to the jails came in a quiet moment of prayer. No one was more surprised than me. Six years into my recovery, I felt the pull into something deeper, something more than just regular Sunday church attendance. In recovery, I had learned something of what it meant to truly be of service to others, and for the first time in my life felt that I knew what it was like to have a real primary purpose – that of staying sober and helping others. I had made a good start at understanding the nature of the trauma inflicted by alcoholism and drug addiction, both my own and that of the family I grew up in. Through the Twelve Steps, I was beginning to experience real healing of my troubled spirit, which was hard inner work but necessary. I was beginning to embrace a new way of being. And now I felt God was beckoning me even further, deeper. I wasn't sure what it was all about, so I prayed and I talked to trusted friends and priests. I prayed that God would help me understand and open doors that could show me the way. What happened next occurred in a moment I will never forget.

One night as I sat quietly in prayer, something felt different. The stillness seemed deeper, the silence profound. I felt the nearness of my Creator, calm and yet vital. Then a question came that seemed to rise from a depth of truth within me. My question to God was this: "What do you want from me?" That query seemed to hang in the air with mysterious energy. Then out of the stillness I felt the whisper of God's response: "I need you in the jails." It was clearly and undeniably God. It wasn't audible (I've never actually heard the voice of God), but it was *felt* in a truer listening space within me. This was one of the most intimate moments I have ever experienced. I sat in silence in my little prayer area in my small apartment in Burbank with the icon of *Jesus of Sinai* gazing at me in the dim glow of candlelight. The icon depicts the two natures of Jesus. The left side of his face is firm and challenging, while the right side shows his gentle, loving nature. It was real and it was penetrating. I was stunned, and in a way, terrified. But it felt right. On one hand Jesus was asking me to do something that was not at all easy. On the other hand, I was comforted in a way that is hard to explain, but I knew that God was with me and guiding me in truth.

✦ ✦ ✦

Although many of my stints of being locked up had been largely uneventful, my last two in L.A. County Jail were horrifying. I witnessed things that were branded in my memory and on my soul, things that evidence the worst of what humanity can be. Now I sat in this safe and sacred space with God, being asked to return to that place. I truly wanted to do my best to turn my will

Jesus of Sinai

and my life over to God, but why the jails? Why me? Eventually, more – much more – would be revealed. But in that moment, even in the midst of fear and trembling at the idea of stepping into what God was asking of me, I had a strange steadiness and confidence that God knew what I could not know, and I trusted where I was being guided. So, with some deep breathing and a few moments to gather and settle myself, the words came: "Yes, Lord. Here I am." It was a moment of obedience and surrender to God's will and from that moment on, nothing would ever be the same.

And so came my invitation to a fuller, more meaningful life. It wasn't expected or even welcomed with enthusiasm. Instead it was surprising, if not shocking, and seemed like a radical notion – to step back into the last place I would ever have chosen for myself. My jail experiences had left me wounded and triggered memories of even earlier wounds in my life. What on earth was God up to? And yet, I was able, even in the midst of all the apprehension, to somehow muster up just enough willingness to follow God's will for me, albeit with unsteady steps. What I thought at first was stepping into bad memories and the worst of what humanity can look like has instead led me to a place where I continuously witness the best of what humanity can be. Over the past fifteen years I have become more sure-footed, and yet sometimes my steps still falter. Sometimes I stumble, as do my incarcerated friends. It is those divine companions living in exile who have taught me so much about walking, and falling, and getting up again.

I never dreamed that sitting in that small prayer corner would lead to such a life, one that I wouldn't trade for anything. It has now taken me into myself and beyond myself in ways that are nothing short of spiritually breathtaking. That night, the invitation came to a fuller experience with God through connecting with who Jesus referred to as "the least of these who are my family."

I invite you into this sacred journey of discovery through struggle and grace with some of the most beautiful people I have ever known – our incarcerated brothers and sisters. They have much to offer in style, kindness, decency and dignity under some of the most trying of circumstances: our jails and prisons.

✦ ✦ ✦

I, the Lord of sea and sky
I have heard my people cry
All who dwell in dark and sin
My hand will save.

I who made the stars of night
I will make the darkness bright
Who will bear my light to them
Whom shall I send?

Here I am, Lord
Is it I, Lord?
I have heard you calling in the night
I will go, Lord
If you lead me
I will hold your people in my heart.

—Dan Schutte

CHAPTER TWO

Exile

By the rivers of Babylon—there we sat down and there we wept when we remembered Zion. On the willows there we hung up our harps. For there our captors asked us for songs, and our tormentors asked for mirth, saying, "Sing us one of the songs of Zion!"

How could we sing the LORD's song in a foreign land?

—Psalm 137:1–4

Those caught up in the cycle of incarceration have been knocked around by life. Most, if not all, were first victims themselves, but lacked the resources and opportunity to heal from their trauma. It is not surprising, therefore, that the cycle would continue from one generation to the next. Hurt people hurt people. The conditions that contribute to incarceration include racism, poverty, abuse, addiction, violence, mental illness, homelessness and inadequate education. Family systems are often permeated with such dynamics. Young people in such environments are never taught proper life skills to cope with adversity and challenge; instead they learn to strike out and to become the aggressor. Many, if not all, grow up in shame. Many grow up without fathers. Others are shown unhealthy models by parents who themselves were caught up in the same cycle of trauma. It's cyclical and generational. It becomes the expected norm, the lot in life.

My own family was imprisoned by the four dreadful demons of poverty, alcoholism/drug addiction, domestic violence and child abuse. There was no encouragement for anything such as college or career. It was unspoken, yet understood, that ours was a life of struggle followed by early death by addiction. For my parents' generation, that meant full-blown alcoholism. In my generation, drugs were added to the fatal mix. It felt like the family curse. My uncle Bobby Gene was fifty-one when alcohol took him out. My mother Evelyn was fifty-eight. My uncle Tommy was thirty-eight. My cousin Ricky was twenty-four when he died of an overdose.

For some, the weight is just too much to bear. My dad's brother Joe was thirty years old the day he stood in the back yard, placed the barrel of a shotgun under his chin and pulled the trigger. It's unnerving that my cousin Morrie was that very same age when he ended his own life in the same way. And yet, the family remained strangely silent about the devastating cycle of alcoholism and general insanity of it all. This life was the only life we knew, maybe because it was just too much hard work to crawl out from under the rubble. But it can be done. I have done it in my own life. I have, by God's grace, been able to break the cycle and seek healing and freedom from the shame that hovers like a cloud of secrets in the life of exile.

✦ ✦ ✦

Similarly, the people I have met behind bars have been judged, condemned, branded as "bad" and largely discarded as unworthy and unredeemable. They have been pushed around by the circumstances of their lives and pushed aside by the mainstream. They have been banished to the wasteland of our jails and prisons, out of sight of the larger community. This is large-scale exile. It's called mass incarceration. The Los Angeles County Jail System, which now houses people sentenced to prison terms in addition to those in the court process, has an inmate population of roughly 18,000. It is the largest mass incarceration facility in the world.

On a national scale, according to the *2017 Prison Policy Initiative Report*, the American criminal justice system holds more than 2.3 million people in 1,719 state prisons, 102 federal prisons, 901 juvenile correctional facilities, 3,163 local jails and 76 Indian Country jails as well as in military prisons, immigration detention facilities, civil commitment centers and prisons in the U.S. territories. These facilities are filled with our societal failings. Because of our inability or unwillingness to properly address the real issues of racism, poverty, addiction and mental illness, we instead try to hide these failings in our jails and prisons. We try to incarcerate our way around the problems, at the cost of human dignity and life.

Many of those living in exile behind bars have known other forms of exile in their lives before they were ever locked up. And the same is true for those lucky enough or privileged enough to avoid incarceration. Those who have been abused as children – whether physically, sexually, or emotionally – know what it's like to live in the exile of shame. I know from experience about the lonely desperation of addiction and homelessness. Women (and men) who have suffered from domestic violence know of the prison of silent shame, fear and sense of powerlessness. People living in poverty know what it feels like to stand outside the mainstream; sadly, most first realized it as young children. Mental illness brings with it a challenge to find one's place in a world that can never fully understand the silent struggle of isolation and confusion. And racism is a corrosive and shameful thread that continues to eat away at the very core of our common humanity. Slavery has never been abolished in our country; one need only step inside any jail or prison to see clear evidence of this truth. My good friend and a retired bishop in the Episcopal Diocese of Los Angeles, the Rt. Rev. Chet Talton, once said that "racism is America's fundamental sin." Sadly, this is as true today as when I first heard him say it.

All of these forms of exile are tributaries that feed into the ocean of mass exile behind bars. So just how *do* we sing our song in the alien soil of exile that is the prison-industrial complex? How do we lift our voices that speak of the struggle, the heartbreak, the joy, the brokenness, the grace and the beauty of life in exile? In Sister Greta Ronningen's book *Free on the Inside – Finding God Behind Bars* (Cathedral Center Press, 2017), she describes one of the most important elements of healing wounds: to first find a safe and sacred place to tell our story. In order to move from brokenness to healing and wholeness, we must be able to tell our story in a safe and sacred space of compassion and love. Many of the friends I have had the honor to walk with during their time of incarceration tell me that they have never had anyone really listen to them. They have never had anyone value what they had to say. That is why our ministry is primarily one of *compassionate presence and holy listening*. Sometimes the stories are spoken from our lips, and sometimes our tears are our words. This is about speaking truth and seeking truth. It's about pulling the harps down from the trees and singing our song, and we sing this song together.

Another essential element of true restorative justice is a welcomed return to community. Our story is about getting to know people in new ways and inspiring a depth of love and compassion for the "stranger" in our midst that can inspire flourishing in community. It's about all of us returning from exile, not just those behind prison walls. We all have our own prisons; all of us are exiled in little ways, or not-so-little ways. Our journey is about coming home – all of us.

✦ ✦ ✦

The Four 'N 20 restaurant in North Hollywood is a small popular eatery known for its pies. It's one of those places that is better known by the locals than by the millions of tourists who visit Los Angeles each year. Other than the pies, the menu's offerings of burgers and the usual diner fare is not bad, but nothing to write home about. The charm and attraction of the place is not so much the menu but the history. It's been there for decades and has become a connecting place for old friends and a gathering spot after the various 12-Step recovery meetings in the area. I know, because for years I drifted in and out of those meetings in what Alcoholics Anonymous calls *countless vain attempts* to gain a foothold in recovery. The Four 'N 20 is also located on Laurel Canyon Boulevard in the North Hollywood section of the San Fernando Valley where I hustled dope and roamed the streets during the last seven years of my life in active addiction before I was able to get sober and allow myself to be rescued by

God and the program of recovery. My darkest times were here in this land of oblivion between 1991 and 1998.

I had been sleeping behind a small, run-down office building on a large-box piece of cardboard for a couple of weeks. It was hard and cold, but relatively safe. It was one of many spots where I would hide away for the night. One morning I woke up – or should I say that I *came to* – with the usual hungry stomach and sick with craving for alcohol and dope. I did what I had done a hundred times before: I searched out a supermarket to lift some booze and maybe food. That morning I decided on Gelson's on Laurel Canyon across the street from the Four 'N 20. I had my routine. I knew what to do, and I was pretty good at it. I would go in, grab a basket as if I were a legitimate shopper walking the aisles, toss a few things in the basket and along the way stuff a couple of tall boys (16-ounce cans of beer) into the lining of my jacket along with some packaged sliced ham and small tortillas. As I casually left the basket and headed for the door, my heart rate quickened, partly from the risk of being caught, but also in anticipation of being able to pop those tall boys and get my morning medicine.

Just as the automatic doors opened and I stepped out, there was a rush of activity and two security guards tackled me to the ground. I was busted. They led me back to the security room of the store and began the interrogation and humiliation. What was my name? Where was I from? Why did I steal? To my surprise, they didn't call the police. Maybe they just felt sorry for me because I was so pathetic. Instead, they had me sit with the tall boys, ham, and tortillas in my lap, and they took a picture of me sitting there dirty, with my stolen goods. This is the exile of shame. They told me to never come into their store again and they let me go. I walked out into the street, still sick and needing something to quell the craving. I walked across the street and past the Four 'N 20.

There was a row of tables and chairs inside the restaurant, right next to the window on the street side of Laurel Canyon, only about six feet from the sidewalk. I had sat at those same tables before my life went into the toilet. Now I stood outside, looking at a man and woman sitting there comfortably eating, laughing, and enjoying their slice of life. They seemed happy and content. Standing there on the sidewalk just a few feet away watching them, I longed for their life. My heart ached at the feeling of being so lost. Even though it was just a thin piece of window-glass that separated us, I felt a million miles away. Then suddenly, the couple turned and looked at me, clearly uneasy that I was staring at them from the other side of the glass. I looked away. I walked away. More shame. This is life in the exile of addiction.

In over twenty years of recovery, I have stopped in at the Four 'N 20 many times. I always try to sit at one of those tables next to the glass as I drink my coffee and eat my sandwich, sometimes with my friends in recovery. I remember that day all those years ago when I felt so lost and buried in shame. The supermarket is still there across the street. Keeping my promise, I have never been back inside.

CHAPTER THREE

IDAHO

L os Angeles is a long way from Nampa, the small town in southern Idaho where I grew up. And in most ways, the two couldn't be more different. L.A. is a sprawling metropolitan area home to more than ten million people. My hometown was built around agriculture with a population of about fifteen thousand in the 1950's and 60's. Los Angeles is the entertainment capital of the world, whereas our claim to fame in Nampa was the *Snake River Stampede Rodeo* that came to town once a year. L.A. is home to Disney Concert Hall, the Dodgers and Lakers. The entertainment options in Nampa were the Pix Theatre, the drive-in, and the bowling center. There is something to be said for small-town life. It has its own sort of simplicity and charm and doesn't seem as inherently corruptible as life in the big cities, though that may be an illusion.

But there is also a sub-culture that exists in big cities and small towns alike. It is a shared reality that is true whether urban or rural, wealthy or poor, or whether the population is ten thousand or ten million. A certain percentage of humanity will always be plagued with alcoholism and drug addiction and the associated dysfunctional behavior that goes with it. The fabric of my family was saturated in booze, and the effects were obvious no matter how much we tried to hide it, and the corrosive thread of shame ran through it all.

✦ ✦ ✦

Dennis Gibbs

Photo courtesy of Dennis Gibbs

I suppose the summers in my small southern Idaho hometown in the early 60s were like those in most small towns. It was a time for playing baseball, riding bikes, swimming and various ways of adventure to pass the long days under summer sun. Why then was I, a seven-year-old boy, stuck sitting with my siblings in this car parked outside of the Topper Tap Room?

The Topper Tap Room was a dingy little dive, not a bar for the casual glass of beer or occasional cocktail with a friend, but a place for serious drinkers. This was a bar for people so intent on their drinking that they would leave their children sitting outside in the car waiting, and nobody in that bar even considered there was anything wrong with that, although the suspicious glances of those walking by said something else. The Topper Tap Room was a bar for drunks who had their priorities straight, and we were left outside waiting in the car, in the middle of summer.

I remember our sense of dread as the car pulled into the parking space in front of the bar. I knew what the next few hours would be like. The parents always gave the same promise – they were only going in "for one." My mother would bring Cokes to the car to pacify us, or maybe to assuage her own sense of guilt. Maybe she knew deep down that this was a shitty way to treat her kids. But alcoholism doesn't care about that. Alcoholism has its priorities.

Every hour or so, Mom would appear with another couple of Cokes with the promise of "just one more." With each appearance she was increasingly drunk. Any protest we might raise was met with the threat of what would happen if we left the car. I felt inconvenient. I felt like a prisoner. I felt as invisible as the glass through which I stared, looking at another world outside of that car, a free world. I didn't have the words for it in those days, but I know the words for it now. It was alcoholism. It was child neglect. And it was wrong.

Were you there, God? Were you sitting with us in that car outside that dirty little bar?

The color of racism

The Spencers were the only black family in my home town, and they lived a couple of blocks away from us. I liked them. They had a large family and although we had the common experience of life in poverty, their house had something ours didn't: a joyful and loving spirit. I was drawn to it like the thirsty are drawn to clear water. Two of the boys, James and Charlie, were my friends. We would play basketball outside at the school until the sun went down and we couldn't see the rim to shoot. Some of my best memories are of shooting baskets in the cool night air.

My dad wasn't too keen on the Spencers and didn't want me hanging out "down there," which was only down the street. He never gave a real reason for it, but I knew even then it was racism; I just didn't have the word for it. This was the 60s, and some of the kids at school hurled insults my way and called me "nigger lover," though that never stopped me. But what James, Charlie and their family endured was much worse. One night, we arrived at their house after shooting baskets and learned that someone had left a bag of human shit just outside the front door and lit it on fire, hoping that whoever opened the door would try to stomp the fire out and step in the mess. But the Spencers didn't fall for it because, sadly, they had seen it before. They also had seen racial slurs scrawled on the sidewalk in front of their house. One day, Charlie told me that they were moving away. I never saw him or his family again. With time, people forgot about the Spencer family, but I never did.

✦ ✦ ✦

We were always poor. My dad had a steady job, but our poverty was brought on by our parents' alcoholism. We were poor because they spent much of their time and money in the bars drinking. It was a depressing existence where alcoholism seemed to rule the day and determine the future. It felt like a sub-standard way of life and, although we may not have said it out loud, it shaped a sub-standard way of seeing ourselves. It created a lower expectation of what we might be and what we might become in the world, and in some way, I know that it affected our perception of how God saw us. It was subtle, but it was there. The world didn't think much of us, and we didn't really think much of ourselves, so why would God be any different?

My mother was a basically a good-natured woman, although when she was drunk she would become pathetic and embarrassing, or downright nasty and mean-spirited. Alcoholism does that to the best of us. But at her core she was a good, loving person. One of the nicest enduring memories I have of her is the kindness she showed to the men who rode the trains. The railroad tracks were just about a hundred yards from our house, and there was a campsite nearby for those traveling through. Some of the men (I never saw a woman rail rider in those days) would camp out for a day or two before continuing on because they had to keep moving or risk harassment by the local police.

I was ordered by both my parents not to go near that campsite, which meant, of course, that I was there often. I loved hanging out and talking with the men, hearing their stories, and watching them make food and coffee over the fire. Sometimes I would have a bite to eat but the coffee was horrible. Some people called them bums or hobos, but to me they were fascinating, and it felt exciting and adventurous to be around them. At the same time, I could see their struggle. Most, if not all of them, were alcoholics. These men had taken some hard knocks that had landed them out of the mainstream. I would listen to their stories and they would ask about mine. They actually listened to me. We had a mutual interest in each other, even though I was just a kid, and I always felt safe with these so-called outcasts. They felt like my kind of people.

When they showed up at our house, my mother would have them wait at the back door while she made them a sandwich to take with them. I learned that the rail riders had a system to communicate to those coming after them which houses were welcoming and which ones were hostile. It turned out that our house was one of the good ones, and that's how the men knew to go there. They even somehow knew they should go to the back door. They were always polite and grateful, and my mom was always kind and generous. I felt good knowing that kindness was being offered to the world through that back door, because life inside the house was pretty messy at times.

As I recall watching while my mother served up sandwiches and dignity to those men, I know the seed of compassion was planted within me by her. God's grace can sometimes be found between the campsite on the tracks and at the back door of hospitality.

The God Imprint

I was considered a pretty good kid growing up. That's what I've been told, anyway. My memories of my earliest years are spotty, which is common for kids who grew up in alcoholic and abusive conditions. It seems harder for me to locate the pleasant memories than the unpleasant ones, but they are there. One of those memories is of my maternal grandmother. Cleda was a tall, broad, big-boned woman from Collinsville, Oklahoma, where she had raised my mother and her four other children before moving to Idaho. She was a devout Christian woman and never drank a drop of booze. In the midst of the dark swirling winds of alcoholic family dysfunction, she stood firm in her faith and her love for God. She was truly the light on the hill, although that hill may have seemed far, far away at times. I can still hear her voice saying, "I pray every day that all of our family will come to know the Lord."

She never preached at me, or dragged me off to church. I don't think I ever spent a day sitting in the pew with her, but I watched as she quietly gave herself to the love of her Lord Jesus Christ and she showed that same love to me and others. She remains to this day one of the most influential evangelists of my life. During my early turbulent years, she instilled in me a three-fold truth: that God was real, that God loved me, and that God was always with me. This certainty has remained with me throughout my life. Even in my darkest moments – and there have been many – I have never doubted this truth. It has, in fact, saved my life.

✦ ✦ ✦

Boxing with God

It was winter in Idaho in 1964. I was nine years old and curiously drawn to a church not too far from our house. The people there were different from those I was accustomed to. They were kind to me and I felt welcomed and safe, so I kept walking to that church on Sunday mornings. I don't remember ever going inside for services. I think I may have been afraid that if I got too close someone would ask too many questions that I didn't want to answer, such as where my parents were. My parents weren't much for church. They spent a good deal of their Sundays sleeping off hangovers, so no one really noticed that I began walking by myself to church. I don't recall thinking too much about it. It was more that I felt a pull in that direction and I didn't really question it. It just felt right. Looking back on it, it was more intuition than anything, although I didn't know about such things then. But I did trust how I felt about the place and the people there.

They were kind and attentive. It felt safe. So I kept walking to that church on Sunday mornings.

That's how I found myself at the Trailblazers Group on that Tuesday night, February 25, 1964. I remember it well because it's my earliest memory of making a real connection with God. The Trailblazers were the church's version of the Boy Scouts. The leader of the group had suspended the regular program for the evening in lieu of something big broadcast over the radio. There I was with about ten other young boys, and we were all crowded around the radio, listening with eager ears as a young, brash boxer named Cassius Clay fought to take the world heavyweight title from Sonny Liston. We pressed together, leaning into the sounds of the fight coming through the radio with ten-year-old fascination and excitement. I had never felt so much part of something, so much like one of the gang. I was just like them and they were just like me. For the first time in a long time, I was happy. In that moment everything was perfect.

As I leaned with my ear to the radio, my line of sight traveled across the room of that church basement to the pale yellow wall … and the cross. As our little crew of Trailblazers was captivated by what was happening though the radio as Cassius Clay pulled off the thrilling upset, I was transfixed by the cross on the wall. That's when I made the connection: this was about God, who loves us, who welcomes, us, who cares about us and protects us, and in whom we can find joy. This God says that you are fully and equally loved, like all of the other kids. Like part of the family. All of that came in one moment, with my ear pinned to a radio, enthralled by a young boxer and mesmerized by a cross on a wall.

God meets us where we are in life – even a nine-year-old boy trying to navigate through a messy young life and finding himself in a church basement boxing with God. God's grace is like that sometimes.

✦ ✦ ✦

My parents were divorced when I was thirteen. It had been brewing for a long time. It was a Sunday night, and my sister and brothers and I were all in bed. Even before then, the tension between our parents permeated our young lives, and there were many nights when the drunken fights would keep us cowering in our beds like prisoners. But this night was different.

My mother came home drunk after having been gone all weekend. My father was yelling accusations – "You've been with Elmer again!" I knew he was right. We all knew that our mother had one affair after another, though we didn't talk about it openly because it brought so much shame. Our mother left that night and never lived with us again, abandoning her children for booze and sex.

Millions of children are deeply wounded from abuse and neglect and live in fear of their alcoholic parents. But my brothers and sister and I didn't know that in 1967. Hiding in our small dark bedrooms, we felt alone. It felt like the Psalmist's warning: "Be alert! The devil prowls around like a roaring lion looking for someone to devour." But now I know what I didn't know then, as the Psalmist goes on to say: "... many of your brothers and sisters are undergoing the same type of suffering."

After that night, any sliver of hope that there would ever be anything close to a normal family life was dashed. My father spent almost every night in the Topper Tap Room, which was around the corner from the lumber yard where he worked. We would usually see him early in the morning, but only then, because every evening after work he would make that walk around the corner to that bar. My older brother, Bobby, dealt with the craziness by spending most of his time away from the house. Who could blame him?

With our father staking his claim on the barstool and my brother old enough to escape with his friends, that left me to care for my sister Peggy, who was seven, and my younger brother Russ, who was just three years old. Not that anyone officially gave me that responsibility; it was more because no one else seemed to be paying attention. So each day, the three of us would do the best we could to keep it together. Each morning we would walk three blocks to Mrs. Reynolds' house. She had a sort of day care she was running in her house. I'm not sure if it was official and certified and all of that, but it was safe and she really loved children. We would leave Russ there for the day, and then my sister Peggy and I walked on, first to her elementary school, and then I would continue on to Central Junior High where I was in the seventh grade. After the school day, we would reverse the trip and all go home to dinner, baths, and bed. We were too busy just trying to survive this strange new life to really know just how messed-up and unfair it was. But I know what it was now. It was abandonment. It was neglect. It was alcoholism.

I have heard it said that what doesn't kill you makes you stronger. One good and enduring thing that came out of that time, as the three of us clung to one another in survival mode, was that a special bond was created between me and my sister, who was old enough to actually remember those fragile times and those walks every morning and afternoon. Although I was only thirteen then, I was her big brother and her protector.

About thirty-five years later, I mailed Peggy a birthday card with an image of two kids about the same ages we were back then. In the picture they are walking down a road away from the camera. The boy has a gentle, reassuring arm around the shoulder of the younger girl. Inside the card I wrote, "Some things never change."

Curiously, even though we were in a struggle to survive something we didn't even understand at the time, the recollections of those walks with my little sister and brother were the last pleasant memories of my younger years. Shortly to follow was the beginning of what would become a real-life nightmare.

✦ ✦ ✦

Seemingly overnight, my father remarried. When his new wife moved herself and her three daughters into our house, it felt like something out of a movie where terrorists come in and take control of everything. She wasted no time in commandeering our house. She was filthy and she checked-in at about 5-foot-8-inches and about 250 pounds. Her daughters were all three chips off the same block. My father was still checking out by drinking every night at the Topper Tap Room. My brother Bobby checked out in his own way. As for me, I felt stuck. My stepmother and I never got along, ever. Although she treated my younger sister and brother somewhat better, she was horribly abusive to me and Bobby, first emotionally, and then physically. I was angry and defiant. She wasn't my mother. Who did she think she was to run riot over our house and boss me around? There is no doubt that I added fuel to the fire. But I was thirteen and I was confused and scared. It wasn't a fair fight.

One summer day she came after me hard. I ran. She chased me out the front door of the house. It was like one of those nature shows on television where the predator is closing in on its prey and you almost don't want to look because you know it won't be pretty. I could easily have outrun her, but I tripped and fell down the front steps of the house and it was over. Once she was on top of me it was all I could do to minimize the damage. The fight dragged out into the street. It didn't take her long to leave me sprawled out on the asphalt, with marks that would soon become bruises and blood splattered on the front of my white t-shirt.

After I shook off the daze, I realized I couldn't go back into the house, so I decided to walk the four blocks to the lumber company, where my dad was at work. Kids normally turn to their parents in time of trouble, but ours was no ordinary family and I remember my trepidation about how my father might receive me. I was right. I walked into the front door of the lumber yard offices barefoot and bleeding. My dad looked up from his desk and immediately bolted to his feet and came toward me. Oh, how I needed for him to kneel, put his arms around me, and comfort me, not caring what anyone thought. These are the kinds of fantasies many abused children have.

Instead, he grabbed my hand in that way he had grabbed it before when I was in trouble with him. He marched us to the back of the place where no one could see us. I started to say something about his wife beating me up, but he silenced me (another common occurrence in child abuse). He told me to never, *never* walk into his workplace and embarrass him like that again. "DO YOU UNDERSTAND?" he snarled. I nodded and watched as my tears hit the floor.

I did understand, but not in the way he wanted me to understand. What I understood was that compassion and love for his son would never come before his need to look normal in front of others. The truth was that as soon as he left that job every day, he went to the bar until closing time, when he would stumble home drunk. I understood that my father made a choice that day and he did not choose me. I understood in that moment that I had absolutely nowhere safe to turn. I also understood that our relationship as father and son would never be the same. I now understand, some fifty years later, that the shame of his own life was projected onto me that day and it resulted, as it most often does, in scapegoating. In a way, he didn't have a choice, because to be honest with the world about himself would be too much.

I left that day through the back door in shame. I never walked into his workplace again.

✦ ✦ ✦

Not long after the street fight and the scene at the lumberyard office I decided to move in with my mother and her lover, Elmer. I never had a good feeling about Elmer and the whole situation with him and my mother, but it seemed like the only alternative. It was the summer before my sophomore year of high school. I was angry and confused and had a bad case of "Fuck It All." I started to drink and use drugs. First it was pot, but soon turned to acid and speed. I was fifteen years old. That's when I made the choice to jump, as it turned out, from the frying pan directly into the fire.

That night

My instinct about Elmer was right. My mom had tried to paint a picture for me about how much better it would be to live with them, but the image didn't last long. They spent most nights out and would come home late after the bars closed. They were always drunk and loud. I hated it. I hated the drunkenness. I hated the smell. I hated the fact that my mother so easily threw away her dignity and self-respect. My mother had gotten pregnant after meeting Elmer and had a child when she was forty-two. I was often left to watch Kelly while they were out at the bars, shirking their responsibilities as parents. I hated them for being so cavalier and reckless. I was seventeen and most always stuck at home babysitting. Friday nights were the worst.

Even after my mom had promised I could go out with my friends, she would saddle me with babysitting, showing little regard for any plans I might have for a Friday night out. When I got home from school she would inform me that she was meeting Elmer "downtown" (that was code language for the bar) and they were only going to "have a few." My heart always sank with disappointment and anger because I knew she was lying, even if she couldn't know it. It always turned out the same. I would sit waiting for hours, watching the clock and hoping that somehow this time it would be different and I would be able to join friends at the movies, or a football game. But it was never different and they would eventually stumble in drunk in the early morning hours, either laughing or yelling and fighting. More often, it was the latter. Elmer routinely beat my mother, knocking her around, dragging her by the hair, kicking her. When I tried to defend her, I would get my share of it. Many nights after these beatings I would gather my mother off of the floor, clean her up and lay her down to sleep. It filled me with anger, sadness, pity and shame. More than once I thought of how I might be able to take Elmer out.

Sometimes people would be with them, like my uncle Bobby-Gene, who would pass out on the couch in the living room and offer the opportunity for me to dip into his wallet for a little extra pocket money. Stealing the money felt like a sort of revenge for the way I was being treated and a way to reclaim a momentary sense of power.

As bad as this day-to-day existence was, soon our world would be shattered by violence like I had never imagined before or experienced since.

✦ ✦ ✦

It was a Friday night. Same routine. My mom and Elmer were out drinking and I was stuck in the prison of our house babysitting my one-year-old half-brother Kelly while all of my friends were out having fun without me. But there would be nothing routine about the outcome of this one.

This night it was my mother, Elmer, and my uncle Garry who burst into the house drunk after closing time downtown, oblivious to the fact that we were sleeping upstairs. At first it just sounded like the usual loud drunken bullshit coming from the kitchen. I listened from my bed. Then the tone changed. Things became more intense. My heartbeat quickened. Although I couldn't see it or make out what they were saying, I could sense the danger like an aroma wafting through the house. I didn't want to listen but I couldn't stop from listening. The words became more threatening, and louder. As much as we were used to these angry drunken arguments, this somehow felt different. Elmer was yelling. My mom was slurring drunken accusations. My uncle Garry's voice was part of it. I was scared, mostly for my mother, who always got the worst end of it. Then all of the sudden things went quiet.

I heard my mom talking in lower tones. Someone was talking with her, but I couldn't tell if it was Elmer or my uncle Garry. My mother may have been crying. If the other voice was comforting her, it was surely my uncle's, because I never heard Elmer comfort anyone in any way. Why were there only two voices now? Had Elmer left? Had my uncle left? I didn't know what to do. Part of me wanted to go downstairs, but who knew what I would walk into? Part of me wished I could just simply fall back to sleep. The talk was quiet now. I listened closely. Nothing. Maybe things had ended peacefully.

The explosion was deafening: the sound of a large gun blast, glass shattering and instant chaos. Screaming, followed by another gun blast. More screaming. Elmer's voice was the loudest now. I started to lose it. God damn! I knew this was bad. Real bad. I didn't know what to do. Should I go downstairs? Should I hide? What about my mom? Kelly started to cry in his crib. I picked him up and started holding him and rocking him. I heard my mother wailing uncontrollably and screaming. I started to cry and pray the only way I could, saying, "Please, please, no, no," just wanting it all to go away, though I knew it was real and wasn't going away. I heard a car pull out of the driveway and looked out to where Elmer always parked his car. It was gone. I put Kelly back down and ran downstairs. I guess I figured his crib might be the safest place for him.

My mom was on the floor beside her younger brother, who had been shot in the abdomen. There was a lot of blood. Broken glass from the front door was everywhere. My mother looked crazed. Drunk and sobbing, she said, "The son-of-a-bitch tried to kill us." As she held her bleeding brother, she yelled for me to call the police. She would later tell them that there was an argument and that Elmer had gone out to his car, gotten a deer hunting rifle, and blasted through the big glass door before swinging around and taking aim at her, but Garry had stepped in front to shield her when Elmer fired the second shot that hit him in the gut. He saved my mother's life and almost lost his own.

The rest of the night was a blur. Garry was taken to the hospital. The police processed the crime scene. My mother was a mess. Elmer was on the run. The sun was rising. People started to arrive. I'm not sure whether they were there out of genuine concern or a morbid sense of curiosity. My hunch is that it was both. Someone took Kelly home with them. No one was sure what Elmer's next move might be. The police seemed to think that he was probably trying to get as far away as possible to avoid prosecution for multiple counts of attempted murder. As it turned out, they were right.

After that night, as much as I wanted to stay with my mother, I knew that I couldn't. I knew that she was surrounded by more capable hands than mine, should Elmer make the mistake of returning. My mom's family was a tough bunch, and I knew she was safe with them. I moved out the next day. As I walked out onto the front porch, I saw Kelly's little plastic toddler Hot Wheels tricycle with blood spattered on it. It seemed disturbingly surreal and sad, a macabre symbol of who we had become.

One doesn't recover from such trauma quickly or easily. Even to this day the images – the sounds, the smell, the emotions – are all seared into my memory. These types of events shape your life and how you see the world forever. Sadly, the large majority of those who have suffered such trauma never find their way to the difficult and tender work of healing from wounds that cut so deep. When I was able to get sober at the age of forty-three, the path was finally set. The recovery I have found in Twelve-Step Spirituality laid the foundation for a wider plane of healing work that has continued since that time. The work has been deep and tender and brave. It is primarily the work of compassion – first for myself and the young boy who sat alone for so long with the wounds, and later for others around me, including those who inflicted the wounds. It is the most important work of my life and it is setting me free to truly love.

Twin Falls County Jail

It's hot standing on the side of the two-lane highway. The summer sun is relentless, beating down like it has some kind of personal vendetta. There's not much along these long stretches of road between southern Idaho towns. Just sagebrush and a farmhouse off in the distance. Every so often a car comes whizzing by. Most pay no mind to our outstretched arms and hitch-hiking thumbs.

This is a conservative part of the west and our thumbs aren't the only things standing out. The long hair, the bell-bottom jeans, the beads hanging from our necks ... all of it sends a message that we aren't interested in conforming to the norms or bowing to the establishment. It is a message that we are proud to carry in our reckless youth in 1972, but it isn't serving us so well on this desolate highway as cars – one after another – pass by with indifference broken only by the occasional suspicious stare.

My friend Duane and I had set out earlier that day from Nampa feeling adventurous, with only the clothes on our backs and no destination in mind. For us it was the expression of freedom. But now, as we stand melting into the dust on the side of the road, it feels more like a misguided eighteen-year-old's impulse, although neither of us want to give in and say so. The thin rubber soles of my tenny-runners offer little insolation from the scorching heat rising from the asphalt, so I'm standing on the edge, in the gravel. It's not much better. We start and stop walking in the direction we are headed, then start and stop again, waiting, hoping, for the ride that never comes. The shadows become long as evening arrives and reality starts to set in. Could it be that we will never get a ride through this pathetic expanse of nothing? The silent scream of desperation from within me pleads "God, help us!" It's the sum total of my prayer life in these years.

Our silent desperation is interrupted by the far-off sound of a car coming down the highway. I can see the car coming through the translucent heat waves rising from the highway. We watch it come toward us with cautious optimism. The last twenty cars have passed us by, so we aren't too quick to get excited.

The two girls in a beat-up Chevrolet slow down and come to a dusty stop on the side of the road, just ahead of where we are standing. An arm launches out of the passenger window waving an invitation, and we start running toward it. I can hear Creedence Clearwater Revival blasting as we get closer. As I approach the passenger side, the driver turns the music down a notch or two and the girl in the passenger seat looks at us and says, "Where ya'll goin'?" We point in the direction the car was headed. "Get in," she says with a flirtatious smile.

As we climbed into the back seat, the inner voice is quieter now. "Thank you, God." I don't know if God actually sent two cute girls in an old Chevy to pick us up that day. More likely it was coincidence, good timing, or just plain luck. In just a few hours, though, I would wish that they hadn't stopped to give us a ride.

✦ ✦ ✦

Although I couldn't articulate it then, I know now that growing up under the oppressive veil of dysfunctional behavior brought with them layers of shame, guilt, anger, and an overall sense of desolation. It was like trying to walk with a pile of bricks on our shoulders bending us over so all we could see was the ground. It's sad for me to think of my siblings and me carrying the weight of this dreadful existence. We were all so young and innocent. We were victims of our circumstances and none of the adults seemed to notice, or they simply and sadly couldn't because they were lost in their own fog. It felt like there just wasn't anywhere to turn, and in fact there wasn't. Clearly, the choices my parents had made in life were poor ones, and choosing those who would become our step-parents made things even worse. Those choices were never made with in the best interest of their children but instead in the best interest of alcoholism and addiction to sex. This was equally true for my father and my mother.

I did the best I could to get through the next few years. I discovered some coping tools to help me along the way: first pot, and then speed and hallucinogens like LSD, mushrooms, and as always, alcohol, to help numb the pain and block out the reality of my life. The drugs and alcohol became my friends in the midst of the unrelenting stormy weather of my life. In a very real way, I think those early years of drug and alcohol abuse may have even saved my life. It's interesting now to think about how the very thing that once helped me get through the days and nights would in the end almost kill me.

I couldn't wait to leave Nampa. That's how I found myself hitchhiking to Twin Falls with my friend Duane.

✦ ✦ ✦

The girls, Sandy and Kris, were in front while I was in the back seat with Duane, rolling a joint. John Fogerty's voice was belting out an endless stream of Creedence hits, the girls were laughing as we passed around a quart of beer, the car was barreling down the road. Things had taken a turn for the better and the flirtatious glances held the promise of good times ahead.

The sun was setting by the time we rolled into Buhl, Idaho – a small nothing of a place about twenty miles out of Twin Falls, which was the biggest town in the area and the county seat. Sandy lived in Buhl, and the plan was to stop at her house before heading on to Twin Falls. We had stopped at a liquor store and Duane bought more beer with his fake I.D. We had decided that it was better for him to go in alone as his chances were better if he didn't have three other underage misfits with him to arouse suspicion. We knew about small towns and how things get noticed. Duane returned to the car with a case of Budweiser and we went on our way. So far, so good. Or so it seemed. The girls took us to a spot a few miles outside of town that was a popular hangout for drinking. As it got darker, they suggested that we move the party to Kris's house. She assured us that her parents were gone for the weekend and we would have the place to ourselves. So off we went.

We were within a couple of blocks of the house when we saw the sheriff's cruiser behind us. Instant panic set in. All of us were under the legal drinking age, we were drunk, in possession of alcohol and drugs, and now the cops were on our tail. This could be bad ... very bad. Just as we pulled into the driveway of the house the lights started flashing behind us. The siren yelped. I saw Duane stuffing speed and weed in the cracks of the back-seat where he was sitting with one of the girls. But there was no way to hide the beer and there was no hiding the fact that we were all ripped. As if things could be any worse, Kris informed us that her dad was a county sheriff's deputy.

Buhl's population couldn't have been more than a couple of

thousand, so of course the few deputies who patrolled the area knew the families of their law enforcement pals. Seeing these two girls cruise through town with a couple of strangers in their car was cause enough for suspicion and, legal or not, cause to pull the car over. We hadn't broken any traffic laws that we were aware of, but this was small-town America in 1972. These towns had their own rules.

We went to jail. The girls went home to face their parents, deputy father and all. I'm not sure whose fate was worse. Duane did a good job of stashing the dope, so it wasn't found during the search of the car. The formal charges were *Minors in Possession of Alcohol.* The informal charges were *Two Lousy Good-for-Nothing Wanderers Partying with the Deputy's Daughter.* I don't remember ever being given a field sobriety test, which may account for the fact that we weren't charged with being under the influence.

Buhl was small enough that they actually had to have someone open the city jail in order to book us. The jail shared space with the fire department, so there was a big red fire truck parked outside our little cells. In the morning we were served hamburgers from the local *Arctic Circle* hamburger stand. It was all kind of amusing in a small-town sort of way, like something out of *Mayberry, RFD.* The next day we were transferred to Twin Falls and sentenced to thirty days in county jail. No longer amusing. Bigger jail. Tougher scene.

Like many who experience jail for the first time at a young age, I was afraid. I was dropped into a small dorm of a bunch of men, all of whom were older and more experienced at this than I. This wasn't some high school game anymore. This felt more hard-core. All of the sudden I didn't feel so cool. I felt more like a sheep among wolves, but I couldn't admit it. I'm pretty sure the guys in the dorm saw through my bravado. Some of them messed with me a bit for their own amusement, but a couple of the older inmates took care of me and helped me along. This is a pattern that would repeat itself over the many jails in many cities I would "visit" over the years. In these jail environments you learn the value of aligning yourself with the right people.

There were about six or eight of us in the dorm and we spent most of our time sleeping, reading whatever was available, playing cards and just talking a bunch of crap to each other. It's amazing the amount of bullshit that is tossed around a jail dorm. There's lots of talk about how inmates have it all figured out, lots of jailhouse prophecy. There is story after story of the unfortunate and unfair twists of fate. Many inmates see themselves as victims of their circumstances, and I have found that to be true, but not in the sense that one may first think of. And of course most everyone was innocent, or at least they claimed. And most all had grand plans about what they were going to do when they got out of jail this time.

There was one older guy there who was really torn up. You could see he had put on a lot of hard miles in his life, and it was hard to tell how old he was because a lifetime of alcohol and drugs had taken their toll. One of his arms had been amputated just below the elbow and he had a flap of skin that hung down about four inches beyond the stump and he walked around without a shirt all the time. You could see his ribs covered with a thin sheet of pale skin, a sunken-in face with eyes that looked like caves and that damn piece of skin hanging down and flapping around. He looked desperate and dying. I felt sorry for him.

One day as we were all sitting around flipping cards and telling our stories, the one-armed man seemed particularly agitated. He had always seemed to be on a desperate edge, but this time he was wound tighter than usual. He was pacing back and forth the length of the dorm like a caged animal. With each trip he got more intense. He was talking to himself and the more wound up he got, the louder and angrier he became. The tension was thick and everyone was on alert. A couple of the guys tried to get him to settle down a bit, but that only made it worse. Then all of the sudden, he ran the length of the dorm and just before he reached the end, he lowered his head and rammed into the concrete wall like a pile-driver. The dorm erupted. Everyone jumped up, cards flew off the table, we were all yelling. Some stood back in horror. Others ran to the one-armed man, who was knocked out cold, with a major crack in his skull. Blood was everywhere, splattered on the walls and pooling underneath his limp body. I watched as the emergency personnel came and eventually took him away on a gurney. I never saw him again.

It was a long time before I would know how to speak about that day in the jail. I now know that in the mix of fear and panic, I also cared about that man. I was experiencing compassion. Now, that might not sound like much to a lot of people, but it was a big deal for me. For many the connection with compassion is a natural one, but not for a person like me, who had grown up in an environment of addiction, violence, and shame, where every day felt like I was fighting for my life, physically, mentally, and emotionally. I had become so caught up in survival that I couldn't be sensitive to the suffering of others – I just didn't have the emotional bandwidth. So this moment when I felt the flow of compassion was big for me. It opened a space within me that had been closed off and forgotten.

The memory of that first jail experience has stayed with me for all of my life, partly because of the shock of the first time being locked up and the horror of the attempted suicide, but also because in the flood of terror and confusion, there was an unmistakable awareness of real compassion for another suffering soul. That day helped me rediscover the place within me that was – and is – out of the reach of all the bad stuff, untouchable by darkness. It's the place where God dwells within us. It's the divine ember that softly burns within each of us, fueled by love. God's heart was breaking for all of us that day. God was weeping for us and with us in that smelly, dingy jail dorm.

✦ ✦ ✦

Father, father

I hadn't seen Duane since we were in court the day we were sentenced, so after being released from jail, I headed back to Nampa alone, this time on the bus with a ticket I bought with the few bucks I had. The moment we started rolling I started feeling uneasy. Going home was not a pleasant thought for me. The scene of the crime wasn't behind me in Twin Falls where I was arrested and jailed that first time; it was ahead of me in my own home. With each mile the feeling of dread tightened its grip. My hope was that maybe I could crash at a friend's place for a few days until I could figure things out. The two houses where my family members lived were not home to me. I knew that I couldn't count on my parents for anything. I was in it alone. It's a strange and confusing paradox to have parents living and within reach, and yet feel like such an orphan.

I don't remember where I stayed after returning to Nampa. Most likely my reentry was quiet and uneventful. It wasn't all that uncommon for me to disappear for short periods of time, and even though I had been gone for a few weeks this time, I'm not sure anyone even realized I had been gone.

I had mailed my dad a letter from jail a few weeks earlier. I didn't hear back. No surprise. That letter to dad, like many I would mail over the years until his passing, was a feeble way of reaching out in hope for something beyond my reach – a father's love for his son. Throughout my entire life, my father couldn't say the words I longed so deeply to hear. I yearned for some kind of action, some gesture, that would express what he couldn't with words, but it never came. There was never a phone call, never a birthday or Christmas card. I made those calls and mailed those cards and letters, always hoping to inspire a response that would never come. The closest he ever got was when, in response to my words "I love you, Dad," he would awkwardly say, "Okay."

I often wondered what it was that had closed him off. What had happened in his life to cause the shut-down? What was it like between him and his own father? We never had the opportunity to have those conversations. For some reason, he had walls around him that could not be breached. For many years I was angry and frustrated. But I also had my part. I too began shutting down in my own alcoholic isolation as the years progressed.

✦   ✦   ✦

Many, if not most, of the men living in exile in jails and prisons have some type of "father wound." Either their fathers were completely absent from their lives or they were negative role models. Some were abusive. Sadly, it is rare to meet an incarcerated man who has a healthy father-son relationship. Just as sadly, the great majority of women incarcerated have been sexually assaulted by men, often family members. I can never know exactly what it's like for the men I sit in friendship in jails. But I can deeply relate to our common experiences. I know what it's like to feel orphaned by a father who is sitting in the same room. I know what it's like to feel invisible and unimportant. I have heard it said that the opposite of love is not hate. It is indifference. I know what it's like to feel the silent sting of such indifference, and so do the men with whom I share this common experience. I know the terror and powerlessness of watching my mother being beaten by the raging hands and feet of my step-father Elmer and then have that violence directed toward me. Many of the men I sit with in our healing circles know it all too well for themselves. The external wounds are visible and obvious. The black and blue bruises, the cuts, the broken bones all are outward and visible signs of an inward and invisible disgrace of shame and humiliation.

My natural father was not physically violent like my step-father. The internal wounds came from trying to be in a relationship with a man who couldn't connect– for whatever reason –on any emotional level, who neglected his children and failed to protect us from an abusive step-mother. Through it all he remained largely silent. The few words he did speak were too often those that carried with them diminishment and shame.

I was a bed-wetter until I was about ten years old. Today I know it was due to the emotional insecurity and fear that comes with an unpredictable and volatile household. My father's solution was to try to "break me of it" by shaming. He would proclaim loud enough for all to hear, "He's just too God-damn lazy to get up at night and go to the bathroom." Sometimes I went to school smelling of urine. The shame was unbearable. These wounds may not be visible, but they are deteriorating to the soul. They are the signs of shame and humiliation. If a young person hears these words and takes enough blows, eventually the lie begins to take root – the lie that you are something other than beloved by God.

When I was just six years old, I was sexually molested by a family member. I carried that silent shame with me for the next forty-five years and it permeated every area of my life. It was only when I was able to confront my sexual predator as an adult and speak my truth that the shame began to loosen its grip. It's been a long road of healing, and it has not included any contrition on the part of the abuser. He is still in a prison of his own making, but today I am free.

✦ ✦ ✦

In the summer of 1973, I was back home in Nampa after another hitch-hiking trip to Seattle. That's where I met Kathy. After I sneaked her out of her home in the early dawn one morning, we hit the road and thumbed it some five hundred miles all the way back to Nampa. I was nineteen, she was seventeen and we were living in a crappy little trailer that couldn't have been more than 150 square feet. We had those square carpet samples of all different colors patchworked together over the floor. It looked kind of crazy, but hey, it was the hippie heydays of the 70s and almost anything went, right? And yes, there was the lava lamp, standard issue for every little hippie home. We were rudderless and stoned most every day, listening to the likes of Grand Funk Railroad; Crosby, Stills, Nash & Young; The Moody Blues; and Alice Cooper. We were broke, but we were free and happy. Those were the best years of my early life.

One day, I decided that I needed to look for a job. It was long before the Internet would change our world, and the only way to find jobs, other than word-of-mouth, was searching through the classified ads in the employment section of the local newspaper.

I just had one problem. I didn't have a newspaper. So I walked the three small blocks to my dad's house to see if I could borrow his newspaper to look at job possibilities. When I walked up, my dad was outside tending to his garden. I said hello. He said nothing. I tried again. "Hi, Dad!" Without looking up he said, "What do you want?" I explained that I was looking for a job and I was hoping to borrow his newspaper for a few minutes to see if there were any listed I might try out for. Still not even looking up, he said something that struck like a dagger.

"What does it matter, you'll never amount to anything anyway. I don't have time to get you the paper."

I stood in stunned silence, unable to speak. He kept looking down. I felt like I had just been kicked in the stomach. There was nothing to do but turn and walk away, so I started back up the street feeling empty and alone. What I didn't know at the time was that I would begin to swallow the lie he had given me that day, and that the walk away from that moment would be more than two decades long. Every time I took a drink the voice would be with me. *"What does it matter, you'll never amount to anything anyway."* Every time I would score another bag of dope; every time I lost a job; every time I went to jail; that voice was there. *"What does it matter, you'll never amount to anything anyway."*

It was forty-three years later, with eighteen years of recovery, that I was finally able and willing to do the necessary work with my spiritual director that would set me free. It is the work of the compassion practice that allows us to cultivate and nurture compassion for ourselves that can lead to healing of these wounds within us – in this case, the wound of those words, so unfairly inflicted upon that nineteen-year-old, words that I carried for so many years. The breakthrough came when Frank guided me in meditation around this wounded place within and I found myself beside that nineteen-year-old, walking down that sidewalk that day. I asked what he needed. The answer was that he needed a loving hand and someone to walk with him. So I did. With my arm around the young hippie, we walked away from our father tending his garden. I felt real and deep compassion for the young man, but I also felt deep compassion for the father left behind. We both turned to look back to him now. He was standing with a sunflower he had pulled from the dirt and he was holding it out, offering it to us. I took it. With tears running down my face, I said that I want to be the sunflower in my dad's garden. And indeed, in that moment I was that sunflower. I know that my dad is looking down from Heaven all these years later, seeing things as God sees them. He sees his sunflower. He sees his son. And I see him. Now there is only love.

CHAPTER FOUR

Movin' on

Geographics is a term we use in recovery that refers to running from place to place, from city to city, in order to escape the circumstances of our life and the consequences of our addiction, always under the illusion of a new opportunity and fresh start. I know now that it was really just me running from the truth of who I was. My need to escape carried me away from Idaho and to six cities and four states in eighteen years, eventually bringing me to Los Angeles, setting the stage for the biggest shift in my life. But as there can be no Easter without Good Friday, the darkness of my night would last a long time before the sunlight of the Spirit could break through.

After that summer afternoon at my father's house in 1973, his words – *"What does it matter, you'll never amount to anything anyway"* – were still ringing deep within me when I set out with Kathy, my young pregnant bride, for the Nevada desert. We were excited about a new job I had been promised and the adventure of the move. But all of this was a mask for something darkly dysfunctional going on. What I am about to describe may sound like pure insanity to those who haven't lived under the lash of alcoholism – not just its denial, fear, and false hope, but also the selling out of one's soul. I believe these are the handiwork of the evil one. Under the influence and control of such dark power, people like me do things that we would never dream of doing in our right mind.

It had been two years since the shooting and Elmer's escape into the darkness that night. It turns out that for reasons I will never fully understand, charges were never brought against him by Garry, the only one who was shot that night. It was clear, however, that Nampa was not a safe place for a drunken coward like Elmer. Two years had been long enough for my mother to be seduced into following him to Las Vegas and taking up their life together again as if nothing had happened. What a paradoxical trap she was in – not able to resist the very person who struck terror in her heart. The drive for sex, the thirst for alcohol, was too much for the rational mind that might scream out against it. This is the insanity of addiction.

It was under these bizarre and unthinkable circumstances that my mom made a connection with a family member in Nevada who held a somewhat influential position with Union Pacific Railroad. She convinced him to hire me. So, putting all my best thinking aside and with our denial in full gear, Kathy and I set out for the Nevada desert for my new job as a gandy-dancer in Arden, Nevada, twenty miles west of Las Vegas. The thought of being in the same vicinity as Elmer made me queasy, but the fact that I was desperate for a job made me go forward. But something within me knew the truth: I was going to Nevada to protect my mother. I think she knew it too.

It wasn't long before an end came to Mom's relationship with her abuser. She had fallen so far under the control of prescription medication and alcohol that she was in a constant fog. When I realized this, I made the choice to call our family back in Nampa. Within a week or so, my uncle Bobby-Gene and my aunt Julie arrived from Idaho with a pickup truck and horse trailer. We waited for the following Saturday morning, when we knew Elmer would be at the corner bar for a few hours. Our plan worked. It only took about two hours to get my mother and half-brother Kelly moved completely out of the house, including the furniture. It felt like sweet revenge. As my mother sat in the passenger seat of the truck ready to roll, she looked at me with the dazed and confused look I had come sadly to know. She asked, "Where am I going?"

I simply answered, "Home." She was finally free.

Gandy dancing

> **gandy** (gan-dee) **dancer.** noun, *Railroad slang*
> 1. A member of a railroad section gang that lays or maintains track.

Gandy dancing is back-breaking work. This was the mid-70s, before the automation of track maintenance on the railroad would change how things were done. For me, the work was long days under the hot sun out in the middle of nowhere in the vast Nevada desert. It was old-school hard labor. I was nineteen years old when I arrived in the spring of 1974 to begin my work with the Union Pacific Railroad, starting at the bottom, at the job no one wanted. I was desperate. Job prospects in Nampa were bleak at best. Higher education wasn't even remotely in the conversation with my family, so the options were limited.

Arden, Nevada was a small section town for gandy dancers on the mainline between Las Vegas, Nevada, and Los Angeles, California. There were five houses where the section crew lived with their families. The house we were in was small; it was basically a square box walled into four equal size rooms. There was a swamp cooler in the living room that offered only a modicum of relief from the hot, dry desert heat. The nearest launderette was twenty-five miles away in Vegas. The total population of Arden was eleven. That was it. We worked hard during the day, sweating under the boiling desert sun from above and the melting heat rising from the rails below. At night we drank as hard as we worked.

Our section crew was responsible for maintaining thirty miles of high-speed freight rail that wound through the desert. Long freight trains with thirty to forty cars would thunder across the desert floor at speeds of up to sixty miles per hour, making the ground rumble with hundreds of tons of cargo riding on two rails less than 3 inches wide and spaced about four feet apart. Sometimes the trains jumped the rails, and then we would be called out, day or night. When you have that much tonnage flying out of control, it is always a huge mess, sometimes taking days to get everything back in place so the trains could run again.

The trains were merciless toward anything in their path. Often their victims were animals; it was common to find large dogs that had been hit and killed. Sometimes it was groups of large lizards or a lone rattlesnake. Once we got called out in the middle of the night because a car had been hit at the crossing near our section. The bodies were removed before they called us in, but I'll never forget the sight of a little kid's tennis shoe in the mess of the wreckage. I thought about that tennis shoe for days. I still think about it.

Fridays were the days when we walked track, meaning that each of us was given three to four miles of track to inspect. I walked down the center of the tracks carrying a heavy spike maul (something like a sledge hammer with a long, narrow head for pounding spikes) in one thick-gloved hand and a four-foot-long steel wrench in the other, for tightening any loose bolts I found along the way. I often walked with one heavy steel tool resting on each shoulder. Steel-toed boots were standard issue for this work, so my feet always felt like they were baking inside the boots. The work was dirty and sweaty. I had shoulder-length hair that I twisted up under my helmet, which earned me the nickname "Wolf."

I looked forward to those Fridays walking track. It was a chance to be alone, and there was something about the vastness, the wildness and the silence of the desert that spoke to me. The desert has its own special kind of silence. Everything seems so limitless and wide open. In the expanse of the desert, you can hear a lizard scurry twenty feet away and the call of a hawk floating over the hot tranquil air for what seems like miles. I had hours to just walk and think, or not think. Looking back, I know this was my first contemplative practice experience. I didn't know how to identify such things then, but I knew the felt experience was deep. I was nearer to my true self – my sacred self – on those days surrounded by the desert and feeling at one with everything.

✦ ✦ ✦

Jimmy was a big, broad, full-blooded Native American. He lived next door to us on the section with his wife and young son. He was a quiet man, a sort of gentle giant. I liked him, and we had some good talks in the desert. But something happened to Jimmy when he would start drinking. It made me uneasy to be around him when he got to a certain point of intoxication. Drinking with Jimmy always felt like we were on some sort of dangerous edge. But he was a good friend and I cared about him. One night, Jimmy got drunk and apparently was driving along the access road and rolled his truck down the embankment, killing him. I felt sad for his wife and young son, Notah; they seemed lost in shock and grief. After a couple of weeks, they just quietly disappeared. We never saw them again.

My friend Willie worked and lived on the next section town over in Sloan, Nevada and was a kindred spirit. Many of the gandy dancers were hard drinkers, including me, but Willy and I also shared a taste for good pot and spent many an afternoon and night getting stoned and listening to the likes of The Doors, Bob Dylan and Buffalo Springfield. We both felt like we just didn't quite fit in, like we were always just outside the circle of things. Willie was becoming a real friend. We both loved to drink, and nothing stopped us. Driving under the influence was our norm.

One thing that we didn't have in common were brothels, which were legal in Nevada. Willie liked to visit the ladies from time to time. As for me, not only was I married, but I also just never felt right about it. Even at my young, rather rowdy age, somehow there was a moral compass within me that wouldn't allow it. It may or may not have had something to do with my mother's promiscuous nature – I don't know. Either way, it was God's grace.

One morning I came to work and Vern, my section foreman, told me that Willie had died in a roll-over accident the night before. He had come to my house that evening with a half-case of beer, almost begging me to go with him to Sheri's Ranch, a well-known bordello about forty miles away, insisting that I could just wait in the bar and have a few drinks until he finished his business. I almost gave in but didn't. Willie went off alone that night. He never made it back. I lost a friend. He lost his life.

✦ ✦ ✦

Las Vegas, with all of the glitz of the enormous hotel-casinos with their dazzling entertainments, also has its darker underside of strip clubs, dingy bars and street hustlers. This sub-culture, a sort of modern-day Sodom and Gomorrah, is where the bottom-feeders hung out. It was a dangerous place for a young, angry alcoholic like myself, just turning twenty-one, now of legal age to drink and with full access to whatever I chose for myself. I was a hard worker and good provider for our young family, but I was also prone to blowing too much of our hard-earned money drinking and gambling in the casinos. It was a horrible thing to do to my young wife and infant child. But the insanity of alcoholism doesn't care about any of that. It just wants the next drink, the next fix of booze, dope, gambling or whatever.

Looking back, I find it amazing that I made it out of those three years in Nevada alive. There were many close calls. A couple of times I ran my car off the road drunk in the middle of the desert. Once I passed out at the wheel and careened over a highway divider, avoiding a head-on collision only because the other car swerved at the last second to avoid the crash.

This was how it was in the early days as my drinking progressed. It also spelled the end of my marriage, as Kathy came to her senses and headed back to her family home in Seattle with our daughter, Aimee. Most level-headed people would fight for their family. But I wasn't level-headed. I was on the front end of a progressive disease that eventually would destroy everything important in my life. Nothing was going to interfere with my right to drink. And so I watched them walk away.

In 1976 I spent my last few months working for Union Pacific on what they call light duty because I had injured my back. That's not surprising after three years of hard railroad labor. I was given an assignment as a flagman at a railroad crossing near a construction site in Jean, Nevada. The construction project was the Southern Nevada Correctional Facility. Little did I know at the time the prominence of the role prison facilities would play in my future.

Eventually, I quit my job at U.P. and headed for Seattle, where my daughter was. I made a brief attempt to reconcile with Kathy, but my alcoholism was just too much for her to bear. I eventually got a job as a truck driver for a furniture rental company, and that is where I was introduced to cocaine and entered a whole new world of insanity.

✦ ✦ ✦

One day on my truck route I stopped at a diner for lunch. The waitress's name was Jan. In true alcoholic fashion, it didn't take me long to move things along. Alcoholics by their nature are neither inclined nor interested in delayed gratification. We want it all, and we want it now. Our romance was a whirlwind with occasional thunderstorms. We were married within a few months. Our marriage would last a mere two years, with my alcoholism and Jan's infidelity playing equal roles in its demise. But during that time I had fallen into a job that actually was exciting and held promise. At last.

In 1978, cable television was a new frontier. No one really knew much about it yet. Pledging to get out of a cycle of menial jobs, I somehow fell into work with the collections department of Teleprompter Cable Television in Seattle. My job was to go to customers' homes and either collect an overdue payment or take their cable box. I wasn't very good at it. Most all of the people I encountered were living on limited family budgets, and cable T.V. was their only source of entertainment. I would often walk away without either the box or the money – the business failing of a compassionate heart. That didn't make me too popular with the collections manager, but I was good with people, and the sales management team saw that in me. They moved me out of collections and into direct (door-to-door) sales.

It didn't take me long to catch on, and I quickly became the top sales person in the company. I developed an entire presentation book, complete with movie graphics I had cut out of cable TV guides and magazines. I could cite the pros and cons of regular network television versus cable and to top it off, I had a flair for those kitchen table sales pitches. It was a bit of a P.T. Barnum routine, and when I walked away, more often than not it was with a new cable TV subscriber and a few bucks' commission. I had found my niche. I quickly caught the attention of upper management and became the direct sales manager of the company, teaching others what worked so well for me. As long as sales were booming, eyes were turned away from my drinking, which continued to get worse. There's nothing like adding a little success to alcoholism to make things start spiraling out of control.

I got an offer to follow my boss to Kansas City to build a direct sales team from the ground up. I took him up on the deal, and Jan and I packed up and moved. It was a move I would soon regret. Things started off pretty well, or so it seemed. I was busy recruiting and training good, solid salespeople; sales were starting to roll in; and the company that hired us was over the moon with our success. That's when I discovered that Jan had been having an affair with my boss. I woke up one Saturday morning feeling like I was on top of the world, and by that afternoon I had lost both my job and my wife. Jan got on an airplane to go stay with her sister. I had money and time on my hands, so I did what I knew best. I drank. A lot. For weeks.

A friend who was a salesperson on my former staff snapped me out of my drunken pity party and got me moving in the right direction again. I started sending resumes back to the West Coast, and it wasn't long before I was being flown out for job interviews. I accepted a sales manager position, a kind of a dream job for me. It was in California, where I wanted to be, and the company had agreed to a commission structure I had designed that would pay me more than they were aware of at the time. I had three salespeople from my K.C. team willing to follow me to California, because one thing was never in doubt – I knew how to make money in this business as long as others were willing to turn the other way when I tipped the bottle. The staggering cat had landed on his feet. The future looked bright. I packed my bags yet again and headed out west to my new position at Big Valley Cablevision.

✦ ✦ ✦

California!

As promising as my early entry into California was – in fact, we got off to a rocket-like start – over time, it couldn't bear the weight of my drinking. The sales numbers were there and had a huge positive impact on the company's revenue sheet. All eyes were on this new sales team and its bold young leader. But those eyes were not looking the other way about my drinking, and my cocaine use was gaining speed. Slowly, those who were dedicated to the venture – including my friends from Kansas City as well as some very bright people I had built the current team with – began to see the end game and decided to cut their losses. That's also what the president of the company decided to do the day she sat down with me over lunch and fired me. I begged her to reconsider and professed how much I wanted to work for her. Her response was, "No you don't. You don't want to work for me. You want to sit in the bar every day and drink."

Inside, I knew she was right. It was a humiliating moment of truth. She was also right about firing me. I had become a bad hiring decision and, in the end, a liability. Years later I learned that one of the sales reps from that team went on to become the sales manager, and that two others from my original team had stayed on and they did quite well, following the blueprint we had established. So I guess in spite of everything, some good came out of it for others and for the company. It's comforting to know that.

After my firing from Big Valley, I was only able to only piece together some contract work with small local cable TV companies. I got a gig as marketing director with State TV Cable in Chico, California, to organize a multi-media campaign (newspaper, radio, and television – the Internet was still in the future) to launch a package of new satellite services including ESPN, CNN and MTV. Chico is a college town, so it was a promising launch project. I organized MTV launch parties in local bars that catered to the college crowd, television blitzes, print media, and creative offers that drove up the subscription numbers. Once again, I was a creative force that turned heads, this time on the marketing level. And once again, alcohol and cocaine had their way behind the scenes of it all, and gradually, my drinking and drug problem began to surface. The dew was off the rose.

One day when I went to leave for lunch, my car had disappeared from the parking lot. I was furious and called the bank from my office. "Did you take my car?" I asked the guy who had been trying for weeks to avoid this, giving me one chance after another.

"No," he replied. "We took *our* car." He told me I could come and claim my personal items from inside the car at the towing company. Now I had a problem, and it wasn't that I was out of a car. The problem was that my "personal items" in the repossessed car included a felony amount of cocaine, enough to send me to jail for longer than I wanted to think about. As badly as I wanted that cocaine, I decided not to test my luck by going to the impound yard, fearing that I could be arrested on the spot. I chose to just stay quiet and hope it would blow over. A few very nerve-wracking weeks went by and I never heard from anyone about my "possessions." Nor did I hear from the police. Whew! Another close call.

But things would spiral further downward and eventually out of control. The night of our biggest launch event, with television celebrities in the house and the president of State T.V. Cable in from San Francisco, I ended up pathetically drunk and crawling around on the floor on my hands and knees, searching for a contact lens that had popped out of my eye. It was a pitiable scene that finalized the destruction of my career.

About a month later I was fired. I didn't put up much of a fight. I just didn't have it in me. It marked the end of my career in cable television. A friend who worked with me, with whom I spent many nights partying, sat me down and told me that he thought my real problem was the booze and dope. It had come to the point where even those with whom I drank and used drugs thought I had a problem. It sucked, but again, I knew it was the truth. I had known it for a couple of years. I knew in my innermost self that I was an alcoholic and a drug addict. I just didn't want to stop. Or maybe I couldn't stop. A pattern had also begun to emerge. The crashes were becoming more severe and getting things back together was increasingly more difficult.

✦ ✦ ✦

My girlfriend Sheri had had enough. I stood outside her open door clutching a suitcase she had put all my things in and a fifty-dollar bill she had given me out of sheer mercy. She was kicking me out of her house and out of her life. I had literally nowhere to go. I had burned all the bridges of trust and friendship, and while I had briefly considered going back to Idaho with my tail between my legs, I just couldn't do it.

So I stood facing Sheri. Even her own alcoholism refused to go to the places mine threatened to drag her into. I lingered there, hopeless and afraid. She stood firm. In a last-ditch effort to appeal to her sense of guilt (a classic alcoholic move), I told her, "You know I am going to kill myself."

She said, "That's not my problem," and closed the door.

I was serious in what I had said to Sheri, and she was right in her response. I spent the next couple of days wandering around the streets and going from one pharmacy to another, buying over-the-counter sleeping pills. I must have collected ten or twelve packages. That seemed like it would be enough. I checked into a cheap motel and went across the street to the liquor store and got a quart of Jim Beam whiskey, like my uncle Bobby-Gene used to drink. There was something strangely ritualistic about it all. I sat in that dingy motel room and started removing the pills from their packaging, one by one. When I finished, there must have been a hundred or more total, all piled up neat and white on the dresser top with the bottle of whiskey.

I stared at the pills and the bottle. A baseball game was on the television. This was the moment of truth. I thought about the shit storm that had been my life, about how no amount of love shown to me by others, or success or alcohol or drugs had been able to relieve me from my despair. My life felt empty, and I felt lost and beyond the reach of the joy and fulfillment that I saw in others. I felt the flames were closing in and that I had been pushed to the edge. I could either be consumed by fire or jump off the cliff. Either way I would die. I was choosing to die by stepping off the edge.

I tried not to think about those who would soon hear of my choice. I wrote a note for the police about whom to contact. There was a pause. Everything went still. I took the first handful of pills and washed them down with a slug of whiskey. I knew I was approaching the point of no return. I took another small handful. Another slug of whiskey. Then another, and another. After a few minutes, the pills and whiskey started to do their job. I had crossed the line. This was it. I became groggy, and my limbs felt like jelly. I lay back on the bed. The sound of the baseball game on TV became garbled and then went silent.

Then ... oblivion.

I woke up to the sound of someone pounding on the door, yelling that it was time to check out. *No shit.* I started regaining consciousness slowly. The empty pill packages were on the table with the nearly empty quart of Jim Beam. The note was there. I recalled only fragments of the evening before.

There was more yelling outside the door, "What's going on in there? It's time for you to leave."

I yelled back, "Okay! Okay!" The voice outside went silent. It took me a few moments to realize that I had not died. This was reality, but I was in a surreal daze and hallucinating wildly. At one point I saw a skinny monster-type hand entering through the keyhole of the door. I staggered to the shower. Under the running water the hair on my body started to gather together into what looked like clumps. I began ripping them from my skin thinking they were leeches. I thought I heard voices from the room and stepped out of the shower in confused fear. I only realized the voices were from the TV once I switched it off. I gathered what little I had into my suitcase and left, leaving the note behind.

I started walking up the busy street. It was a strange cacophony of traffic noise, chaos and confusion. Cars honked at me. I'm sure I was a concerning sight, with my crazed look and carrying my suitcase down the middle of the street. As I walked along, I kept hearing the voices of two little girls, a manifestation of my hallucinatory state. When I would turn toward the sound, I would catch only a glimpse of them before they would duck behind a pole or a bush. This went on for hours. People must have thought I was crazy, looking strange and unpredictable, darting over to the girls behind the poles or in the bushes. Yes. Crazy.

I somehow had enough bearing to make it back to Sheri's house. I peered through the window and saw an old woman sitting in a chair. I stared knocking on the window glass to get her attention, but it was just more hallucination. One of Sheri's neighbors called her office and told her I was back and acting strange. She eventually came. Seeing her was the first thing that seemed remotely normal all day. She asked me what had happened. I'm not sure I could even explain it to her. She called the hospital, and they suggested that she bring me in. Things were starting to make more sense, now that the toxicity of the suicidal overdose was easing up. It had been about twenty-four hours since I sat in front of those pills and whiskey. Sheri assured me that I would not be kept at the hospital and that if I would come with her, she would make sure I was allowed to come home with her. It was a ruse to get me to go along. I spent the next few days in the San Joaquin County Hospital under psych observation, before finally convincing them that I was no longer a threat to myself or to others. I don't remember ever being asked about my alcoholism.

✦ ✦ ✦

My mother died of alcoholism on June 19, 1986. She was just fifty-eight years old. She had spent the last years of her life living in government subsidized housing – in the projects – drinking and sucking on lemons to quell the onset of stomach ulcers from a lifetime of booze. Finally one of the ulcers burst and sent her to the hospital. Her body started shutting down rapidly. They removed her spleen, and the prognosis was dire. I got on the first plane to Nampa with a ticket bought for me by a girlfriend whose disease was co-dependency. The perfect match for an alcoholic and dope fiend. She thought she could "fix" me. I let her believe that.

I hardly recognized my mother when I first walked into the intensive care unit at Saint Alphonsus Medical Center in Boise, Idaho. My mother and I had always been close. Even after all we had been through, I had remained loyal to her and was closer to her than my other siblings. And now here I was, staring at the effects of the disease we both knew too well. I also knew I was staring at my own future. I was filled with pity and sadness. It was too much to take in, so I did the only thing I knew to cope with it: I went into the hospital room bathroom and did a few lines of coke.

When we were alone during those days and nights, I would find myself just watching her and remembering it all; the abandonment, the abuse from Elmer, her alcoholism. I thought about a day, years before, when I watched her as she watched Kelly playing in the swimming pool, and I saw the joy on her face. I thought about the time my girlfriend Sheri flew her to California to see me for my birthday (Mom was nervous about flying and hated airports) and I spoiled it all by getting arrested and thrown in jail. I thought about all those years ago when I would watch her feed those homeless men at the back door of the house. I thought about how she would always sign off a letter or a phone call with "Roses on your pillow." And now it had all come to this.

She couldn't talk, so she would struggle to write short notes. The notes complimented a nurse or asked where someone was or told us to go home for the night. One said, "I need air." Late one night when we were alone, I kissed her on the forehead and was about to leave when she made a noise that stopped me. I turned around and she was writing on a piece of paper. When she held it up, it said "I ♥ U." With tears welling up, I patted my heart and pointed to her. She smiled and nodded the best she could. I turned and walked out before the flood of tears came. That was it. She died before we saw each other again.

✦ ✦ ✦

It wasn't long after that when I made my first serious attempt to get sober. I had somehow landed an entry-level job with a local direct mail company, as an advertising rep. I was good at advertising; creative with good sales skills. But my alcoholism and drug abuse was taking me into uncharted waters. It became common for me to spend entire days at the house of my girlfriend Lisa, snorting lines and sipping vodka instead of making client calls. She was fully *in the game* with me – meaning that she was on board for all the cocaine I could put in front of her. As long as I had the dope, I was welcome and we could just party and pretend we cared about each other. I don't think either of us had a clue what real affection or love meant. The only thing we truly cared about was the booze and dope.

I'm not exactly sure how I ended up in my boss Joyce's office early one morning, long before others would arrive, spilling my guts about my drug problem. But there I was. After denying and defending my addiction for so many years, I now stood there telling her the whole thing – how I was addicted to cocaine and alcohol and had been for all my adult life. I told her I was completely lost and I didn't know where to turn or what to do except that I was there in that moment asking for help of some kind, any kind. I was thirty-two years old and it felt like everything was caving in. The drinking and drug use that had begun seventeen years before as a way to escape all the crap that was happening in my family – in a way a protective mechanism – had far overwhelmed and now ruled my life in every way. I had lost two marriages, promising career tracks, friends, lovers and self-respect. My family was beginning to distrust me and keep me at arms' length. I was angry about my life and scared shitless because I had no idea what would come next. It was like I was in a dark room, running my hands over the surface of the walls, looking for the light switch, in a panic because I couldn't find it, and the walls were closing in. But I couldn't tell anyone all of that. The only thing I could do was sit in that conference room with Joyce and tell her that I was an alcoholic and drug addict and I needed help.

The day I found out that I had been accepted into a 28-day in-patient treatment program, the first thing I did was connect with my dealer, Brenda, and score enough dope to get me through the week or so until I could be admitted. I remember standing in her bedroom telling her that I was going to check into rehab and needed an amount to get me through until then. She simply said, "You're crazy." She was probably right. When she left the room to go to the bathroom, I opened the dresser drawer where she kept the large stash, grabbed a big amount of dope and made my escape. I made it to my car and took off before she figured out what had happened – a clean getaway. This was a large amount of cocaine. It was a reckless and danger-ous move, one that could get me in serious trouble with her and her henchmen. But she didn't know where I lived and I didn't plan on seeing her again. Now I had more than enough to get me through, even being the insatiable pig I was when it came to cocaine. But enough is *never* enough for people like me.

I drove away with my heart racing. Not just because I had made a clean break, but because I had all the cocaine I needed. I planned to use every last bit of it before I was supposed to check into rehab, although now I wasn't fully convinced I would keep that appointment. Scoring that much dope has a way of changing your thinking. Whatever way this cocaine run ended, this would be my swan song. My dad's words were still ringing in my ears: *"What does it matter, you'll never amount to anything anyway."*

When the day came, I had my friend Steve drive me to New Beginnings in Lodi, California. *New Beginnings.* The name itself brought up my defenses. It seemed so naïve. Steve was an old tweeker friend who could almost match my level of drinking and drug use. *Almost.* One night a couple of years earlier, we were towing a U-Haul trailer behind my beat-up 1970 Challenger. The trailer was filled with stuff I had to move from Chico to Sacramento after getting fired from State TV Cable. After an overnight round trip with no sleep and lots of coke and booze along the way, I fell asleep at the wheel. We both woke up with the car careening sideways down the middle of Highway 99. The trailer had twisted loose and rolled into the center median. We scrambled in the dark to get the trailer hitch – which had been torn off the back of the car – dragged off the road, which we finally did. It is a miracle that no cars came along during that fifteen or so minutes. But it was about four in the morning and the highway was deserted at that time. Another close call. But not enough to be a wake-up call.

So Steve was a natural choice for someone to party out my last few days of freedom with. He was reckless and in the game. By this time, I knew I was going to follow through with checking into rehab. It was strange, like I was being guided by God's will, even in the midst of my confused, drug-induced state. I guess somewhere deep within myself and my twisted thinking, I did want to somehow get out of the addiction trap.

I had stayed at Steve's house the previous two or three nights and he was glad to have me as long as I had the dope. I had been awake for a few days straight, doing more coke than seemed humanly possible. We sat in the car outside the rehab facility doing lines, drinking tall-boys and smoking a joint just to take the edge off. Then I did something radical for people like us. I got out of the car, tossed the bag of dope through the open passenger window and said "Have fun!"

Before I turned to walk into New Beginnings, he said, "You're crazy."

"Yeah," I told him, "I've heard that before." I turned and walked up to the entrance and through the door.

✦ ✦ ✦

I walked out of New Beginnings after successfully completing my 28-day rehab. Those first steps into a new sober way of life felt like both freedom and apprehension. During the previous twenty-eight days, I had been occupied with fierce recovery programming and surrounded by people who supported my sobriety. But now I was stepping into the world alone.

All my old friends were part of the drug scene. Calling Steve or anyone else from that crowd was out of the question – that is, if I truly wanted to hold onto my tenuous sobriety. In rehab, I had learned that a large percentage of relapses happen within the first seventy-two hours of leaving treatment. If I could make it over that first hurdle, maybe I had a fighting chance. But the disease was already talking to me.

"Just call Steve."

"What does it matter, you'll never amount to anything anyway."

I had been given a lead on a sober-living house in Sacramento. I stepped into a phone booth and dialed the number. The house manager, Sean, sounded tough and straight to the point. He told me to meet him at the house in 30 minutes.

"Don't be late," he added. Then he hung up. I wasn't intimidated as much as annoyed, but I was strangely grateful, too. There was something about it all that gave me a sliver of hope that I could actually do this thing. I had made the first right decision. I had made the call. I'm sure that there are many who never even make it to that phone call. I'd have a bed and a roof over my head. I caught the bus and went to the address.

I didn't know what to expect when I arrived at sober-living. These were uncharted waters. But what I walked into didn't seem like anything special, certainly not anything like New Beginnings. It was a moderate four-bedroom house about fifty years old. The walls were dingy and bare. The living room was furnished with mismatched furniture, and the whole place smelled like Lysol.

Sean had had a rough ride through life, like a lot of us; he was a few years out of prison and had the prison-yard swagger. But he was a good guy, and I liked him. We would sit on the front porch smoking cigarettes with the other residents in between meals and doing mandatory chores. And there were a lot of recovery meetings, sometimes two or three per day. I eventually got a sponsor, who introduced me to the fellowship while we began working the 12 Steps. I felt like I was truly building a foundation of recovery.

After a few weeks I returned to my job. Joyce seemed genuinely glad to see I was on a good track. But I got no special treatment. I had to start fresh again, which meant that my old territory and list of clients belonged to someone else now. I was sent to Stockton, about twenty miles south of Sacramento. There was *nothing* alluring about Stockton. It felt like being sent into exile. But I made the best of it. I had to remind myself to be grateful and thankful for all Joyce had done for me. I was good at what I did, and clearly even better now that I was sober and wasn't constantly fighting uphill against my addiction anymore. It didn't take long for me to build things back up and begin to start making a reasonable living. For the first time in my entire adult life I felt legit, like I wasn't a fraud.

But the downside was that I was further away from my recovery community. I had to find new meetings, none of which were quite the same. As hard as I tried, I just couldn't find anything I liked about Stockton. I made my gratitude list: I was sober. I had a job. I had an apartment. I had a couple of new friends. And I was apparently slowly being restored to sanity.

Okay, okay … things weren't so bad after all.

Eventually, I was recruited by our biggest competitor, which happened to be the largest direct-mail advertising company in the world. It was a tough decision. I felt loyalty to Joyce and the company I was with, yet this was an opportunity that few in the direct mail business would pass up. So I did the only thing I felt I could do: I talked with Joyce about it. She wasn't happy that the competition was trolling her sales reps, and she also wasn't thrilled about the prospect of losing me. It was hard to imagine that, just less than a year before, she wasn't sure what to do with me and the mess I had become. Instead of firing me, she had made the choice to help me get my life together and career back on track. She had advocated for the company to take a chance on me, and now I'd come to her with this. But she understood the opportunity to advance my career. In the end she not only gave me her blessing, but also recommended that I take the offer. I couldn't help but think that she was a living demonstration of what we learn in the program of recovery: to always place principles before individual personalities. In this case, she was willing to sacrifice her own agenda for what she felt was the right thing to do.

Our parting was difficult and emotional. It was the very first time I had left a company in the right way. I owed a lot to Joyce and it was hard to leave, but we both knew that I had to. Otherwise I would always wonder what would have happened. And what would happen next would be a surprise for everyone, including me.

✦　✦　✦

It was no surprise to most that I got off to a quick start with Advo Systems, my new employer. I did what I had done before, starting at the bottom with a sales territory that nobody wanted and turning it into a revenue stream for both me and the company. I already knew that success hardly ever came overnight. I also knew the value of hard work. I hit the streets and started building a client list, mostly of small mom-and-pop businesses – lots of them. Then larger players came along, and eventually a couple of national chains. Things were rolling. Again.

For the first time, I had a sense of balance in my life. I was sober and going to recovery meetings regularly, showing up for work, and attending St. Francis of Assisi Catholic Parish, where I was eventually, after a year of catechesis, baptized during the Great Vigil of Easter on March 25, 1989. I was 34 years old, and maybe for the first time in my life I was truly happy. Then the unexpected happened.

I was dating a woman who was making a start in modeling – as much of a start in that business as one can make in a small city like Sacramento anyway – and I started hanging out with local actors and models. I loved it. It wasn't long before I became fascinated with acting. Soon I enrolled in acting classes and started performing in small local theater productions. Much like the pattern in my business career, I became the leader of our little pack of amateur actor/models. I started a regular gathering at my place that became known as The Coffee Club. We would help each other rehearse "sides" (parts of scripts) for auditions, practice our own acting craft in various forms, and drink lots of coffee late into the night. And through it all, we were actually becoming better actors.

The acting/modeling school I was enrolled in sponsored me to attend a huge modeling and talent show in Los Angeles. This was long before anything like the TV talent shows that have become so popular nowadays. The IMTA (International Modeling and Talent Association) was held once a year, in both New York and in Los Angeles. I was slated to compete in the L.A. show later that year, entered in six different acting competitions. There were two other actors from our acting community with their sights set on the IMTA competition, and so we went to work rehearsing sides during those coffee club nights, honing the sharp edge that I knew would be required if we were to do well in the competition and be taken seriously in Los Angeles. I had a pretty realistic view of it all and didn't expect much more to happen, other than presenting well and making some connections in L.A. We worked hard and hoped it would pay off in some small way.

Hollywood!

The competition was held at the St. Bonaventure Hotel in downtown L.A. and lasted more than a week. There were all kinds of agencies represented, not only from New York and L.A. but from all over the world, and there were thousands of aspiring actors and models hoping that this might be a break. It was an exhilarating experience. The days were filled with competing in different acting/modeling categories. All of mine were acting; I never remotely considered myself model material, and at thirty-six, I was way too old. I had come prepared, albeit with the natural jitters, but I felt good about the work I did in the acting categories, which were mostly screen tests from prepared scripts and theatrical monologues.

The event culminated in the final night of awards. Of the six categories I competed in, I won four of them outright and placed second in the other two. All of a sudden, things became even more electric in the already buzzing hall. That is when I was invited to join the table at Cushman & Associates, a talent management agency in L.A. Things were swirling a bit. I just went along and said yes, and I was escorted over to the table and given a seat.

The person next to me offered his hand and said, "I'm Mike." I said, "I'm Dennis."

With a chuckle he said, "I know. Everyone here knows who you are now." It was Mike Cushman. He then said, "You *do* know that you just might win the whole damn thing, don't you?" I couldn't even wrap my head around that.

We watched and listened as the ten finalists for Male Talent of the Year were invited to the stage. The seventh name called was mine. It was no surprise to those at the Cushman & Associates table, but it was still unbelievable to me.

Things got loud. Walking up onto the stage – which seemed huge – seemed to take forever. It was almost like I was in a dream. All ten of us stood in a line across the stage congratulating one another on making it this far. Then they began with calling the name of the ninth runner-up. It wasn't my name. Then the eighth runner-up. Again, not my name. It seemed to go on forever, until there was only myself and one other actor standing in front of a cheering audience that we could scarcely see because of the stage lights. It was surreal. I was virtually frozen with nerves and excitement; I was also bracing myself for

DENNIS LEE GIBBS

Photos courtesy of Dennis Gibbs

second place.

And then that voice: *"What does it matter, you'll never amount to anything anyway."*

The place went quieter as the announcer began by saying, "And the first runner up is… " and then he said the name. It wasn't mine! The place went crazy and it was hard to hear over the noise when my name was actually called as "The 1990 Male Talent of the Year."

The next few moments were a blur of handshakes and photographs. Mike Cushman came up and handed me his card and said, "Let's talk tomorrow."

I was swept off to a celebration party hosted in Studio City. I met a few of the past IMTA winners, most all of whom were now working actors. I was still a bit shell-shocked; I really had not expected this. The congratulations were seemingly endless, with recognizable actors, beautiful women and lots of drinking. After the rush of adrenaline wore off, I found myself sitting alone outside on some steps. I should have felt like I was sitting on top of the world. So why did I feel so alone?

Within a couple of months I moved to L.A. to pursue my career as an actor. I got some breaks early, and I had Mike as my manager. It wasn't long before I was working small gigs. I had been cast for under-five work (meaning that your character had under five lines of script) on one of the soaps a few times. At one point I was given the character name of Diamondhead and had a few more lines, which felt promising. I was being cast in small roles in big projects and larger roles in very small films, often playing the bad guy. Once I was cast as the co-star of a short film called *Welcome to the Club*. It was a dark film about an underground Russian roulette gambling racket. I played Tony Gianni, another bad-ass. It was my best work. From the attention of that role, I landed a co-starring role as a troubled cowboy in *Uninvited* – a western thriller and another film destined for direct to video release.

As piecemeal as it was, I was working a lot, and there was some buzz around it all. Mike had high expectations and did his part in getting me into auditions. My media kit promoted me as "a young Tommy Lee Jones type."

All the while, I was enrolled at the Stella Adler Actors Studio in Hollywood. I knew that it would take hard work to create a real break in the business. I was a small fish in a very big pond but somehow found myself working next to A-List actors. I had the pleasure to meet people like Willem Dafoe, Joe Montegna and David Bowie, and had one very brief introduction with the great Lucille Ball. Once during a gig at Sony Studios, Michael Jackson came to our set to visit Madonna. It was amazing. Everything shifted when he walked into the building. I've never felt anything else like it. There was an energy field around him that was captivating and powerful.

✦ ✦ ✦

We had started the L.A. version of The Coffee Club in my apartment in Studio City. It was of course a whole new set of actors, but the work and the intensity were the same. There were a few serious actors in our crew and dozen or so more who just wanted to be part of it all. As in Sacramento, we would work for hours on audition sides and practice methods of improving our craft. That's how I met Kristen. She was a model Mike also represented, and he had suggested she work with us to gain some acting chops to complement her beauty. And she was indeed beautiful. Even in the sea of aspiring models, she stood out from the crowd. She really was something special.

One night, Kristin and I were sitting out near the pool. She pulled out a joint. I hadn't been to a meeting in months. I was sober but by no means in recovery, and I had no defense. She lit it and asked me if I wanted some. I did not hesitate in responding, "Yes." I will never forget that moment. As I was hitting that joint – with the cherry burning just an inch or two from my nose – I heard a voice within me say, "This is going to kill you," but I just kept on sucking. In that moment, everything changed. I was a goner. It was over. Within weeks I was drinking even harder than before and scoring as much cocaine as I could get my hands on. This was the beginning of a seven-year downward spiral into the abyss of addiction that would truly thrust me into oblivion.

CHAPTER FIVE

OBLIVION

It's not dark yet,
but it's getting there.

—Bob Dylan

I t didn't take long for my addiction to take complete hold
once again and begin to dismantle my life. With people like
me who are active in their addiction, it's all about the dope
– getting it, using it and getting more. Everything else becomes
secondary. I began showing up either loaded or hung-over, if I
showed up at all. Needless to say, it was concerning and disap-
pointing to those who had invested in me, especially Mike. It
had truly felt as though we were on the verge of breaking something big. All the pieces were in place, and now this. I was sent
out on an audition for a role that could have brought us closer to
that break, but I was completely out of it and unprepared. The
producer and director had liked me for the part and brought me

back three times, practically begging me to get it together and give them what they wanted.

The part was mine for the taking. But I couldn't do it. I was in too much of a cocaine fog to access the skills that had brought me this far. Years later, Mike described that failed audition as what marked the end of my short career. He said that I had been his brightest and most promising client, only to become his biggest disappointment.

Once, after taping a soap episode at NBC studios, I realized after leaving that I had left a small bag of coke in my dressing room. I rushed back to the studio in a panic because I was afraid they would find the dope when they cleaned the dressing room, and also because I wanted the dope back. I drove as fast as I could. The guard waved me through the gate. I parked and rushed into the studio and down the hall to the dressing room. It was still unlocked.

The bag was gone. Shit!

Something in me knew this was the end for me, and I was right. I never worked on the set of that soap opera again. The phone went silent and so did my career. My last project was *Uninvited*, only because I had been cast before the bottom began falling out. We shot for a month near Yosemite National Park and another few weeks in studio. I was a mess through it all, and the director knew it. But by the time everyone figured out what my problem was, it was too late – there was already too much in the can. This was a low-budget feature film and they didn't have the money to re-shoot, so they trimmed a few of my scenes from the production schedule and did their best to get through it. To make a point, they also removed my photo from all the promotional materials. The film was released in December of 1993, with the opening screening at the Laemmle Hollywood. As usual, I was loaded. It had been just three years since that IMTA awards night at the Bonaventure Hotel. Now my career was over. I never worked as an actor again.

My addiction accelerated at alarming speed, and I became pretty much unemployable. I met a guy who owned a print shop in Burbank, and I worked odd jobs for him in exchange for a few bucks and a place to crash upstairs at night. I spent my days around the shop and nights in The Now Voyager, a bar used primarily for hook-ups and drug use a block away. Every chance I had, I made a run over to the connection for dope. Pretty soon, even this paltry way of living fell apart and I ended up on the streets of North Hollywood hanging out with criminals and junkies. I say that as though I was somehow different, but I wasn't. In fact I was both. I did what I needed to do in order to get the next bindle of coke, even if it was just to get me through a few hours. At one point I got a job at a telemarketing joint that sold toner cartridges. A lot of the so-called salespeople were like me: coke-heads and desperate. I was good enough at selling that I made a few bucks – enough to barely get by and keep a bag in my pocket – but eventually the progression of my addiction ruled my life to the point that I got fired.

I still had a car. It wasn't much. Just a beater I bought for a couple of hundred dollars when I still had that kind of money. It became my home. Everything I owned was stuffed into that tiny piece of crap car. I would move around from location to location around North Hollywood and Van Nuys so I wouldn't attract at-tention. I would usually find a spot on a quiet dark street and set-tle in for the night. I would turn on the car for the radio in short spurts so I didn't drain the battery, usually listening to things like Monday Night Football or UCLA Basketball. The car wasn't big enough to sleep comfortably in. I always slept on the passenger side, away from the steering wheel. Even when I pushed the seat all the way back and reclined it, I couldn't straighten out my legs. I could rarely get more than a couple an hours of sleep before waking up and twisting and trying to extend my legs as far as I could. Then I would remember where I was.

Winter was the worst. I usually didn't have enough gas in the tank to run the engine for heat, so I would run it for just a short time and wake up later freezing. Sometimes I would get settled in and just lie there in the silence. I would look at the houses on the street with lights and life happening inside them – real life. I would see people coming and going – normal people with normal lives. This was loneliness. How did I get here? How did I let my life slip so far away? I wanted to tell myself that this wasn't really me, but this was what I had become. Many nights I would fall to sleep hungry for food and aching for alcohol and dope. There was something about those nights hiding in the shadows. I was like an animal needing a safe place in a dark corner of the night.

I always woke up in the morning jittery and aching for booze and dope, and the craving for those was always greater than my physical hunger for food. Being high on cocaine takes away your appetite, so perhaps my body had long ago adjusted to going without food, sometimes for days. The worst was when I didn't have anything – no coke, no liquor, no food (notice the priorities). Those mornings the desperation of this life was nearly unbearable. After I washed up in a bathroom at a city park or gas station, I would plan my next move of the day. It was usually to head for whoever I thought might have something to take the edge off. On the rare occasions when I had a few bucks in my pocket, getting a bindle was a lot easier. Nothing talks like money in the drug world.

But money or no money, Jack was always a 50-50 bet to help me out with a bump or two. I had started scoring from him when I was still functional and could pay for large amounts. I was a good customer. I was there when his wife, Esther, was diagnosed with cancer and died a few months later. They'd had a volatile relationship, but I would spend time with her, getting high and talking about things. As loaded as we were most the time, we talked a lot about God. I'll never forget that. I knew it then like I know it now, that God was with us even in our addiction.

I had also helped Jack get out of a couple of near misses with the cops when it counted most. He never forgot that, and so I was one of his guys. He knew he could count on me. I was part of the family. But things had changed. Like everyone else, he had watched me slip off the edge. It's a real drag when even your lower companions roll their eyes and lecture you about getting it together. But I could still count on making some kind of deal with Jack to get something to make me well.

One morning I headed for Jack's to see if I could pick something up. We had a rule to always call ahead, which I had done, and Jack told me to come on over. I pulled up and parked a house or two down the street. But something felt off. I noticed that Jack's van wasn't in its usual parking space. I looked around. I could feel it, but I couldn't see it. Maybe the craving didn't want me to see it.

I knocked on the door. No answer. I knocked again. Again, no answer. Now I knew that something wasn't right. My heart started to race as I walked away, and sure enough, as soon as I got to the sidewalk, undercover cops rushed me. Within seconds three or four LAPD officers moved in, with their weapons pulled. I was ordered face down, hands behind my head. The neighbors came outside and started applauding. The police cuffed me and sat me on the curb while they ran the system for warrants. I guess they must have felt that since they had Jack's house under surveillance, that gave them due cause to question me. But even though my intent was to score from Jack, it hadn't happened. I was clean. There was nothing illegal about walking up to a house and knocking on the door, nothing criminal about walking away. I wasn't carrying any dope or weapons, so I wasn't sure just what the "probable cause" was. What it really was, of course, was profiling – making assumptions based on how I looked. My best guess was that they were acting on some hunch or tip and it was bad timing on my part.

Funny thing was, while I sat on the curb with all those black-and-whites and the undercover around, guess who simply drove through the scene like a normal neighbor passing through? None other than Jack! It was the funniest thing. With all the police around, Jack just cruised right through the middle of it all – right under their noses – and all those cops missed it. It was hilarious. Jack and I made eye contact as he rolled by and just kept right on going. It was really something. The one who got away just cruised the party.

As they put me in the back of the patrol car, the neighbors start applauding again. One of the cops refused to use my name, instead referring to me as "piece of shit." I didn't take the bait. It was just a power play because they didn't get the big fish they were hoping for. That was evident by the show of force with a dozen cops, undercover and a couple of SWAT. But all they got was a skinny white dope fiend with a couple of misdemeanor warrants. So off to jail I went, again.

After a couple of days in the Van Nuys city jail, two detectives came in. They wanted to talk about Jack. I didn't want to talk about Jack. One of my warrants was for stolen license plates on a car I used to have a couple of years earlier. They tried to use that as leverage to get information on Jack, saying they could make that charge go away. I didn't take the deal.

In court, I was sentenced to 90 days in County Jail and a fine of $1,000.00. Good luck getting that blood out of this turnip. I ended up doing something like 60 days before being released. I never showed up in court again to pay the fine, which meant the charge still hung over my head. It would come back later to haunt me, as these things always do.

✦ ✦ ✦

Kenny was a low-level coke and speed dealer I had known for a few years, and we had become friends. He was a big fella weighing in somewhere in the 300s. Interestingly, he didn't use much of what he dealt, otherwise he would have become thin like all the others who used regularly. But Kenny *was* a big time stoner. He loved his pot and grew a fair amount of killer weed for his own personal stash. Hanging out with Kenny meant that we would be perpetually stoned, and he would sometimes give me talks about getting off of the hard stuff. He had seen how the very drugs he peddled had destroyed so many lives. We had become friends and I knew that he genuinely cared about me. A few times when I would pledge to give it up, he would refuse to sell me anything when I would come by later, having given in to the craving. But his refusal would only last a few days, and then he would give me what I needed. I guess he figured I would find a way to score anyway and he might as well be the one.

One thing we liked to do was golf the little par-three courses in Studio City and Van Nuys. What a peculiar sight we must have been: Kenny this huge lumbering stoner dude, and me, a tall, skinny coke-head, always with that wild-eyed look. We were an odd twosome on a golf course, but we both enjoyed it.

In the spring and summer of 1997, I was squatting in an apartment with Dean, yet another not-so-low level dealer friend. We saw a constant flow of criminals and people who would do just about anything for the coke, speed, pot or GHP that Dean was moving large amounts of in a circuit of three bars in North Hollywood. Helping Dean in his business was my best chance to get off the street, or at least I thought so. I had become one of his trusted "associates" and spent a lot of time in those bars slinging bindles, and of course, drinking and always flying high on coke. The business was good, but with it always came the risk of getting busted.

That summer, things seemed to be getting tense. There were conversations about a certain woman whom we suspected of being a narc, and by extension, people who were close to her. She had been part of our circle for a while, but then something about her felt different. It was Kenny who had articulated that suspicion to us, saying that she wasn't to be trusted and we needed to be careful. He was convinced that she was working with the cops, and I trusted his instincts. Then someone we knew got busted at a gas station right after scoring some dope. She was spotted at the gas station that day, and we were all pretty sure that she had something to do with the bust. We were nervous after that, because she knew a lot about us from close up. Things started getting crazy and dangerous. Most people were willing to do whatever it took to avoid arrest and prison, and they had weapons. I was in over my head, but wasn't sure how to find a way out. Besides, I had an addiction to feed.

✦   ✦   ✦

It was Friday evening, October 3, 1997 when I got an urgent pager alert. It was from someone who was also one of Kenny's friends. I called back and heard the news that Kenny was dead. He'd been murdered. I would later learn that he had made arrangements to deliver a large amount of crack, but it was a set-up. He was shot through the head as he sat at a stop light at Laurel Canyon Boulevard and Sherman Way. He died in the middle of that intersection, slumped over his steering wheel.

Jim – someone who knew me at the time, but was not part of the drug scene – said, "What did you expect? You hang out with a bunch of criminals and drug addicts." His other disparaging remarks about Kenny pissed me off. I don't think I ever saw him again after that. Even if what he was saying about the life we were living was true, we still at times made real connections with people and formed friendships that were meaningful. We weren't monsters. We were all just so utterly lost and clinging to one another as we drifted in the sea of oblivion. I cared about Kenny. He was my friend, and my heart was broken when he was murdered.

It wasn't long before Kenny's killer was caught and charged with first-degree murder. As nervous as I was about going to court for fear of being arrested, I went anyway. Maybe I was tempting fate – I don't know. But nothing happened. I went for the week-long trial and sat with Kenny's mom, Sally.

I know what it's like for friends and family members of murder victims to sit in court and look upon the person charged with the crime. For me this was a mix of anger and desire for revenge, but also a strange identification, because I knew this guy's addiction ruled his life. I knew that it ruled his life in that moment in Kenny's car. But that was where we differed. He had crossed a line that I knew I was not capable of crossing and I hoped that, by God's grace, I never would be.

Kenny's killer was sentenced to life in prison. It was a dull resolution to such a senseless crime.

Sally asked me to speak at Kenny's memorial service, which was attended by a few family members and friends. I'm not sure what I said. It was a quiet and sad ending. I still think of Kenny and the memories are gentle. He remains with me in loving friendship.

✦   ✦   ✦

It started to feel like Dean and I were keeping only one step ahead of the law. We began moving the operation around to different places, because the bars we had been using felt too hot. We started doing business out of motel rooms that we would rent for a few days before moving on. There was gossip about individuals whom we suspected maybe the cops had gotten to turn. I was uptight. With all this and Kenny's murder, it seemed like we were always on alert now.

One time, we were set up in a motel on Ventura Boulevard in Studio City. I came by the room and found it empty. I had been there just the night before, so I knew something was up. I looked in the parking lot; Dean's car was there. I asked the person cleaning rooms if she knew what happened. She told me that the police had come – lots of them – and raided the motel room. They had taken Dean away. The amount of drugs in the room the night before was substantial, so I knew the bust was a big deal. They finally got Dean, and he would likely go to prison for a long time.

Not long after that "the boys" – the ones who had supplied Dean – came to me. They explained that they needed me to assume Dean's list of customers because they couldn't afford to lose the business. I tried to tell them that I couldn't do it. They said I had to, and then put an amount of cocaine on the table – a *big* amount. They explained that they were going to front it to me and I could pay after I had moved it.

I was nervous. I knew they were nobody to mess with, and getting into trouble with them could be disastrous. But for a coke-head like me, it was an offer I just couldn't refuse. I couldn't wait to taste what was lying in front of me. I made the deal. We agreed to meet in a week or two, depending on how things well things went, to settle up and keep things going.

I called Jack to ask his advice. The first thing he said was that I was the wrong person to be dealing because I was one of the worst drug addicts he had known in this business, and I would end up putting more of the supply up my nose than in the hands of customers. Then he told me that when I got in trouble with the boys, not to go running to him and bringing that trouble to his place.

I knew he was right. I had already dipped into the supply, and it hadn't even been a day. I did sling a few bindles and a couple of eight-balls over the next few days, but now I had both dope and money, neither of which belonged to me, and I was using them as if they did. It was a perfect storm brewing.

My appointment to settle up with the boys was fast approaching. I was out of supply and seriously short on money. I knew that this was real trouble, and yet I was reckless. I started avoiding the boys, not returning their pages. That led to me looking over my shoulder and avoiding places where I might run into them or one of their lookouts.

After both the supply and the money were gone, I started hanging out at Noah's house. He was a low-level street dealer

I had known since my arrival in L.A. seven years earlier. Noah lived in his aging and blind mother's house. She spent all of her time in her bedroom and seemed oblivious to the fact that he had turned the place into a drug den. Or maybe she just didn't want to be involved.

The place was fortified with reinforced windows and doors, and it needed to be. It was a bad neighborhood to begin with, but the drug activity made it necessary to shore up security, as protection not only from the police but from those who might have a chip on their shoulder for whatever reason. I was hiding out with Noah and doing little things – some legal, some not – in order to stay close enough to get a few bumps here and there while laying low, hoping things would cool down with the boys. I was wrong about that.

Meanwhile, the house was a total wreck. Dirty everything, everywhere. It seemed like every inch of the place was covered with crap, and the whole house smelled. I hadn't seen a place this bad since my stepmother had overrun our house when I was thirteen.

Late one night there was some unusual activity outside. There were three of us in the house – Noah, Steve (an old friend of Noah's), and me. As it turned out, someone must have tipped off the boys that I was there; a number of people, maybe six or eight, had surrounded the house, all carrying guns. They shouted that they were there for me.

Noah was quick to act. First, he turned off all the lights in the house. That way, because there were streetlights outdoors, we could see them but they couldn't see us. Both Noah and Steve grabbed guns – loaded guns. Noah took me into the attached garage area. The garage was like the rest of the house: a total mess. Noah had me crouch in a corner and Steve piled dirty clothes over me until I was completely hidden under the stench. I could hear Noah standing his ground during the shouting back and forth. I heard Noah say "You're not getting him. Not tonight." I heard Steve at a different window say, "You make one more move and I'll blow your fucking head off."

I sat under the pile of clothes trembling with fear. Then, something shifted. I felt a presence say, "I have always been with you, and I am with you now." That presence was God. I thought about how my grandmother had instilled in me that God was real, that God loved me and that God was always with me. Even after all the wickedness I had been a part of, even now buried in the darkness of despair under the stench of this pile of dirty clothes, I knew that God loved me and was with me. In that moment, there was stillness. I felt closer to God than ever before.

If I say, "Surely the darkness shall cover me,
and the light around me become night,"
even the darkness is not dark to you;
the night is as bright as the day,
for darkness is as light to you.   —Psalm 139:11-13

The boys didn't get me that night, but eventually they would. I made the mistake of visiting one of the bars we used to hang out in before things got crazy and Dean was arrested. Someone there who knew me told me I had better hurry and get out – a couple of girls who were lookouts for the boys had seen me and had run to call them.

It was too late. By the time I got out the back door, they were waiting for me. I was surrounded by the main guy, "J," and three or four of his crew. "J" spoke first, and I think just out of a weird formality, asked me if I had his money. I didn't. He then informed me that they would be taking my car as payment. I begged him not to. It wasn't much, but it was all I had and everything I owned was in that little car. He didn't budge. He pulled out a knife and said, "I either get the car, or you get this." I knew he was serious. There was no winning this fight, and besides, I was no cowboy. He wouldn't even let me take anything out of the car. He said maybe they could sell the things to help get their money back. Then in a strange but symbolic move, he tossed a bindle at me as they left with my car. "It's all yours," he said.

After that, I went from living in my car to living in my coat.

CHAPTER SIX

New Year's Eve

If I should pass the tomb of Jonah
I would stop there and sit for awhile;
Because I was swallowed one time deep in the dark
And came out alive after all.

—Carl Sandburg, The Losers

It was the morning of New Year's Eve 1997. I woke up to getting beat up in the back of a van. Noah was the one throwing the punches. We had been flying high on coke and cheap vodka for a few days. At some point the dope ran out, as it always does, and everyone crashed. For me, that meant sleeping in the back of the van parked on the street, which wasn't all that bad, considering the options.

The punches jolted me awake. Noah was screaming in my face. I fended off the assault as well as I could for someone who has just been jarred from a drug and alcohol-induced stupor, groggy and for the most part defenseless. Any good street fighter knows the value of the element of surprise, and Noah had me cold on this December morning.

I'd never been much of a fighter, not in the physical sense anyway. I got into a fist fight once when I was in junior high. It didn't last long – I got my ass kicked and that was that. Other than that day behind the school gym, I honestly cannot remember ever throwing a punch at anyone again in my entire life. But for Noah it was different. Beating people, for various reasons, or for no reason, was nothing new to him. I had watched him assault dozens of people over the years. His propensity for violence was disturbing. He seemed to even get a twisted thrill from it all. But I suspect that underneath that mean streak was a deep insecurity. Maybe it was the only way he felt he could get any respect from the world around him, a sense that he was *somebody* and that he had control in his life. The truth was that he – like all of our sad little band of addicted malcontents – was lost. We really had no idea of who we were or how to live in the mainstream. Doing drugs, being petty criminals and scraping the crumbs off society's floor was all we really knew how to do.

Noah finally ran out of punches and left. I stumbled out of the van and looked around. It was early morning, and the air was crisp and cool. I stood there in silence with the taste of blood in my mouth. I wiped the rear view mirror clear enough to see my reflection and inspect the damage. It didn't look too bad, not yet anyway. I knew from my days of being knocked around by my step-father that it would look much worse in another hour or two. I stared at the face in the mirror.

I had known moments like this before, in the mirror of the gas station bathroom that provided me with the closest thing I had to a shower, or haunted by my reflection in a glass window. I was looking at me, but it wasn't me. Not the person I used to be or wanted to be anyway. The sunken features, greasy hair, pale, oily skin ... and the eyes. The eyes were the most haunting – shallow, dark and desperate. Those eyes always revealed the truth about what my life had become.

Standing in the cold that morning, stooping in front of that van mirror, something happened. Even in my dazed state, I somehow knew that if something didn't change, nothing was going to change and eventually I would end up dead. It might come from an overdose, or from my body finally collapsing under the weight of nearly three decades of addiction, or maybe it would happen like it had for Kenny – a bullet in the head. In the end, given enough time, the monster of addiction would have the final say.

Standing there shivering, I knew I had to make a choice. I could continue on the road I was on, knowing that it would lead to eventual but certain death, or I could choose to fight for my life. From the outside, the choice would seem obvious, but I had lived this life long enough that the desperation became what I knew best. I knew the way of struggle. The landscape was familiar to me. What I didn't know was how to find that narrow gate that led to life.

Now I was up against a wall. After all the years of slavery to the bottle and the bindle, the jails and institutions, all the broken promises and disappointments, all the people I'd hurt, on this New Year's Eve Day it was all caving in. My soul was trembling. I was as desperate as only the dying can be. It was a moment of truth. Somehow, I knew that I had to get myself off the streets and away from the people and the life that I had come to know too well. I had run my game on these San Fernando Valley streets for years and now the game was over. The only question was on whose terms it would end.

The bottom I hit was more of a slow burn than a sudden crash, but the landing was still a hard one. After all the years of chasing dope and running from myself, I had come to the very precarious edge of insanity. I was reduced to stumbling around the streets of North Hollywood with a pocketful of cigarette butts, stealing booze and food out of supermarkets. I was clinging to a beat-up briefcase that contained a few memories of a life that had at one time held promise. Or maybe those memories were clinging to me. Either way, the briefcase felt like a lifeline. I had been out of contact with my family for two years – they had, in fact, given me up for dead, assuming I had met my end in some alleyway or something. I was desperately lost, I was drowning in addiction and I was dying. I knew that I was at a crossroads. I knew that I couldn't just stand there and wait for death to take me out like it had taken so many of my friends. So, with nowhere to go, I started walking.

✦ ✦ ✦

I know about walking with nowhere to go. You keep moving, as best you can and as tired as you may be. It's more aimless wandering than walking. I find a nice shady spot under a tree in a city park to rest for a while. I lie down on my back and looked up at the blue sky and the clouds and listen to the birds chirping and singing. I know in that moment that addiction can strip you of your health, your dignity and even your sanity. The world may judge you and push you aside or lock you up, but no one can ever take away the blue skies, the clouds, the singing birds. They belong to me as much as they belong to anyone. I love that about God. It feels good lying here on the grass looking at the sky. It's a moment of peace. I close my eyes and rest. I fall asleep.

I am startled awake for the second time in one day, this time by two LAPD officers. They're loud, and one of them is nudging me with his baton. I slowly make it to an upright position, but stay sitting on the ground. I know the drill. They are asking me what I'm doing there. Isn't it obvious? I'm resting. This is a city park isn't it? Aren't people allowed to enjoy the park and even doze off?

Not if you are homeless. Then you become a nuisance.

The police officers are telling me that someone had called in a concern about a "suspicious" man in the park. As it turns out, I'm that guy. Evidently, people were concerned that I am in the park at the same time as them and their children. I look around. There isn't anyone within 50 yards of us.

They ask if I have any identification. "No."

They ask if I have a place to live. "No."

I'm starting to feel like there's another visit to County Jail in my immediate future. As it turns out, they don't take me to jail, but they do inform me that I have to move on. Turns out that the park isn't for everyone after all. But I still have the blue sky, the clouds, and the singing birds above me, just like those cops and those who expressed their "concern" about me. We all stand under the same sky. But I have to wonder – would they take it away from me if they could?

I get up and start walking again. I've learned since that if you take enough steps in the right direction, eventually you'll end up in a good place.

✦ ✦ ✦

I'm not sure why I chose to head for Chris's apartment that day except that I knew that I had to put some distance between myself and the people I had been hanging out with, and I didn't have many options. Chris and I had known each other for a few years, and the bonds of our friendship were booze and dope. A couple of weeks earlier, I had shown up on his doorstep needing a place to cool down a bit. At the time, I was wanted by both the police and the guys who wanted the money I owed them for cocaine – a lot of money for a lot of cocaine – and I was in trouble in just about every way I could be in trouble. The word of this was out on the street and Chris refused to let me in, saying he couldn't have me or anything that followed me around his place.

But now it was a few weeks later, and I met Chris on his way out the door. He explained that he was headed to the North Hollywood hospital because Tracie, his old girlfriend with whom he still ran around from time to time, was in bad shape. It sounded ominous. I followed him to the car, saying, "What do you mean she's in bad shape?"

"Get in," he said, opening the passenger door.

On the way to the hospital, Chris explained that he and Tracie had been on a run, getting high for a week or so straight and she had gotten sick. He said it might be pneumonia. I felt uneasy. Chris sounded like a boy whistling in the dark to keep his spirits up. I knew what could happen when people got dragged around by the crack pipe and crossed the line.

When we got to the hospital, she had already died.

We stood outside in front, stunned and yet not completely surprised. Death scenes like this are not uncommon in the shadowy culture of addiction. When it happens, there is always the awareness of death's hot breath on your own neck. One day someone like Tracie is part of it all and the next day they are dead. We are all aware, whether we want to admit it or not, that it can happen to all of us and in fact, may only be a matter of time. It's a sobering thought, but it's seldom enough to compel one to get sober.

It's a strange paradox that we instead turn to that same instrument of death as a means to numb the pain of death. As we say in recovery, it's a *heartbreaking riddle.*

I was sad for Tracie. I had first met her at a bar in North Hollywood where Chris and I were regulars. She was fun to be around and one who liked to push the limit. This time, she had pushed it too far. I also felt sad for Chris. As crazy as their on-and-off relationship was, I knew that Chris truly cared about Tracie, even though she took advantage of him. Maybe he took advantage of her too. In the drug culture we're all out to get what we can for ourselves any way we can get it. In the long run, real friendships are scarce and you're usually a friend if you have dope or money. That's just the way it is.

Chris invited me back to his place to get a shower and get high. What else was there to do but to numb out? Not this time. Not for me. I told Chris that I couldn't go back to his place. His look was one of both amusement and disbelief and he said with a sarcastic chuckle, "Where else do you have to go?" I said I didn't know.

It was a lie. I knew where I needed to go. For the first time in a very long time I made a decision that would move me closer to life than death. I wanted to walk toward something, anything, other than the nightmare I had been living. I started walking up Laurel Canyon Boulevard towards an A.A. meeting that I had run across a few years earlier, hoping that it was still there.

I have asked myself what made that New Year's Eve morning different than all of the others that had come before it. The answer is that there was *nothing* different. There was the same desperation, the same sense of hopelessness and aimless wandering and the same awareness of impending ruin. I was painfully aware that I had already begun to die spiritually. I had seen what happened to others like Kenny and Tracie. Why should I be any different? I knew I wasn't. It was a sobering moment. But could I get sober?

Dirty, trembling and dazed from the darkness I had just somehow, after all the years, simply staggered out of, I walked in and sat down in the meeting. The sickness in me was begging me to bolt, but I didn't. Somehow I stayed. Someone brought me a cup of coffee. At the beginning of the meeting, they asked if newcomers would like to identify themselves. I hesitated but then stood up and said, "I'm Dennis, and I'm an alcoholic." It felt liberating to say those words. It took me a few more weeks before I could stop running my bullshit and get honest enough to make a real start in recovery, but eventually I did. I've been clean and sober since and have never looked back.

The day that would change my life began with me getting beat up in the back of a van. Sometimes God's grace looks like that.

CHAPTER SEVEN

The Narrow Gate

Enter through the narrow gate; for the gate is wide and the road is easy that leads to destruction, and there are many who take it. For the gate is narrow and the road is hard that leads to life, and there are few who find it.

—Matthew 7:13-14

The early days of my recovery weren't easy. The claws of addiction were embedded deep. In that first meeting I recognized a guy named Lawrence who I had known from about five years earlier when I was hanging around the A.A. rooms, but still drinking and playing games and not able to achieve sobriety. He didn't recognize me. I had become a shell of my former self, gaunt and thin with the desperate eyes of addiction.

I went up to him after the meeting and said "Lawrence, it's me, Dennis!" He looked shocked, but as if he didn't want to show it. He just looked at me, in disbelief at what he saw. At first he deflected my plea saying he didn't know how he could help me. Who could blame him? I was pretty sketchy. In a whisper,

I begged him, "Lawrence, I'm dying. I need your help. I have nobody. Please ..."

He seemed reticent, but he agreed. "One night. You can stay with me for one night." I felt an immediate sense of ease, like I had just been able to grab a reed to hang onto. As flimsy as it was, it was still hope.

Lawrence took me to his one-bedroom condominium in Studio City. I would be sleeping on the sofa, which was definitely an upgrade from the places I had been sleeping before. Lawrence was going to a sober New Year's Eve party that night and invited me along. I was grateful and willing, so I said yes. Besides, I think we both knew that it was risky for me to be alone. He handed me some of his own clean clothes and pointed me to the bathroom for a much-needed shower. I will never forget that shower. I couldn't remember the last time I'd had had a real one. I must have stood there for thirty minutes, just letting the warm, fresh water roll over me. It was heaven. I shaved with a spare razor, put on those clean clothes and looked in the mirror. I'll never forget seeing my reflection, clean and freshly shaven. My body was quaking, needing a bump or a drink. And I heard a voice: *"What does it matter, you'll never amount to anything anyway."*

Going to the sober New Year's Eve party was agonizing. There I was, toxic with cocaine, booze and who knows what still in my system, surrounded by happy sober people. I felt like I didn't fit in, not yet anyway. People were coming up to me with questions like Are you new? What meetings do you go to? Then when they found out that my last drink was just earlier that day, I got the usual advice. *Keep coming back ... Just take it one day at a time.* I had heard it all before, and though I got it, the truth was that I wanted to bolt. But I didn't have anywhere else to go, so I stayed. It was the most unenjoyable New Year's Eve of my life.

I made it through the sober party and woke up the next morning on Lawrence's sofa. Sober. But my body was screaming, my mind obsessed with how I could get something, anything, to take the edge off. Lawrence came in and said, "Get up. We're going to a meeting." At first he had told me that I could just spend one night, which actually would have opened the way for me to hustle something up. But now here he was, walking in and telling me that if I was going to stay at his place, I was going to meetings. One that day, I guess I wanted to be sober just a bit more than I wanted to get loaded, but not by much. The disease was talking like crazy and I was hanging on the edge of a cliff by my fingernails. I went to the meeting.

It was a New Year's Day speaker meeting at the North Hollywood Group where I had found Lawrence just the day before. The speaker that day was Don M. He was a big presence and a great speaker. For the first time in maybe years, I laughed. The funny thing is, I was laughing about our shared problem of alcoholism. I also cried, which could have been out of sadness, relief or gratitude. Most likely all. People in recovery say that if you stick around long enough you will hear your story. I didn't have to wait long. In many ways, Don was telling mine: the insatiable and insane thirst for alcohol and cocaine, jails, mental institutions and near-death. Like me, he had lost marriages and careers. He had gotten sober sixteen years earlier at the age of forty-one. I was forty-three. I approached Don after the meeting and asked if he would sponsor me. He wasn't quick to say yes. What he did say was for me to call him the next day, and he gave me his number.

The urge to get high was gnawing at me. I knew that Lawrence was on prescription psych meds and quickly learned that it was quite a mixed cocktail. I started sneaking into his supply and taking some of it, without even knowing the effect. The only thing

I did know was that I wanted to get high, which these meds did in a way, but not in the way I really wanted. I was also making clandestine trips to Noah's scoring bindles. Again.

One day it all came to a head and I collapsed. I was taken to the hospital and after a series of denials on my part, the blood test results told the truth. Pot, cocaine, liquor and a potentially lethal mix of psych meds were all on the list. The jig was up. So much for my New Year's Day sobriety date.

To my surprise, Lawrence was there when I was discharged from the hospital and he took me back to his place. It was a show of compassion that I didn't deserve. How could he possibly trust me after all that? How could he have even a shred of hope for my sobriety? But he did, and I found myself back on his sofa. It took some days for my fog to start lifting. There were people willing to drive me to meetings both day and night, even when I was a bit sloshy from my self-medicating experiment. For a few days I was sitting in recovery meetings without being sober. But I know now that didn't mean that my recovery had not begun. In fact, I believe that it had because something shifted in me after that hospital trip. A real honest (imagine that) desire for recovery was brewing within me.

I called Don every day. We would talk about things, and he would end with telling me to phone him the next day. I still just wasn't quite out of the fog yet.

One day I called and we were having our usual chat. Then, Don asked me what day it was. I said, "Tuesday." Then he said, "I mean, what's the date?" Looking at the calendar, I told him, "January 20th." Then he said, "Write it down. It's your sobriety date." I began to weep. After all the darkness and struggle, after all the starts and stops at getting sober, here I was on that Tuesday morning, hearing those simple words spoken with confidence from my sponsor. I was flooded with emotion and I somehow knew things would be different this time. I knew that, even with just that one single day of sobriety, I had made a real beginning in recovery.

✦ ✦ ✦

I started stringing sober days together, going to meetings, talking to Don every day, reading the Big Book and slowly started finding fellowship with others in recovery. Things were going well. I had gotten a telemarketing job selling official-licensed sports apparel, so I was making a few bucks. But there was something weird going on in Lawrence's place. He started nodding off in the living room chair. I couldn't quite put my finger on what felt wrong about that – call it imagination or intuition, but whatever it was, it made me uneasy.

Then one night, it all became alarmingly clear. I came home from a regular Sunday night meeting and he was sitting in the living room with a couple of others – people I recognized from meetings.

They were smoking pot.

I stood there in disbelief as the reality set in. Lawrence looked up at me with glassy eyes and a smirk on his face and said, "Don't worry about it, Dennis, it's nothing." It wasn't nothing. It was bullshit! It felt like the devil himself was in the room. I turned and got out of there as fast as I could, because the truth of the matter was that, for a split second, I wanted to believe him and have a seat and join the party. That's what I knew how to do very well. What I did instead was turn and leave as fast as I could. Totally God's grace.

It was raining outside as I scurried up Ventura Boulevard. I had to pass a liquor store. I stood staring at it, cold in the rain. I could go in there right now and get some booze. There was that damn voice again, *"What does it matter, you'll never amount to anything anyway."* I was getting drenched as I turned and continued up the boulevard.

I finally came to a phone booth. I stopped, pulled some change from my pocket and with hands shaking from the cold rain and the chill of panic within me, I dialed Don's number. He answered. Thank God! I told him all that had happened. He took a moment to help me calm down, and let me know that I had done the right thing and I was going to be safe. He had a confidence about him that was reassuring. He asked if I had a meeting directory. I pulled one from the rear pocket of my jeans. He asked if there was a meeting nearby at that time of night. I was trying to hold the phone and look through the meeting directory, all the while dripping and shivering from the relentless rain. Thumbing through the directory, I found a meeting. I looked at the address. Then I looked at the street sign. Then, I looked behind me.

Amazingly, there was a meeting in the church right there behind me! Amazing grace! Don told me to get into the meeting and call him when it was over. I hung up the phone and ran through the rain to the church. I walked into the basement where the meeting was, just minutes before it started. I took a deep breath. I was safe.

That was February 8, 1998. I was twenty days sober. I wrote this that night on the inside cover of my Big Book:

Step Three – Made a decision to turn my will and my life over to the care of God as we understood God. My God, as I understand God, exists in the program of Alcoholics Anonymous, in the meetings and in the fellowship. Push coming to shove with my sobriety today, I needed God and I knew where to go. My God, as I understand, was in that room of A.A.'s. They spoke to me and they saved my life.

I moved out of Lawrence's place, disappointed and angry but at the same time grateful. Having come off the streets, I had no credit score that could get me into a place, so I ended up renting a weekly motel room in Encino, just about a half-mile up Ventura Boulevard. I called Lawrence from my motel room and told him I couldn't stay at his place, but I was grateful for all he had done for me. He said he understood. I could sense his own disappointment in himself. I wished him well and hung up the phone. It would be the last time I would talk with him. Three months later Don called to tell me that they had found Lawrence dead of an overdose that morning. I would hear later that it was heroin and alcohol. He was found on the same sofa he let me sleep on getting sober.

Lawrence was here for me when I so desperately needed help. I don't know why some of us make it and some don't. I do know that the disease of alcoholism and drug addiction is ruthless in its pursuit of death. But I also know that God's love for us all is just as relentless.

I spent the next eighteen months living in that motel. It was a simple and earnest existence. I went to A.A. meetings every day and my home group was within walking distance, just a few blocks away. My telemarketing job was paying the rent and keeping food on the table. I didn't have a car or even a valid driver's license, so I took the bus almost everywhere I went. It wasn't easy, but it was good. My life was slowly – and finally – getting better.

I made a solid beginning in recovery, showing up for work every day and attending church on Sundays. Little by little, I started to reclaim some self-respect. But maybe most importantly, I was developing a deep sense of gratitude for my life. When you don't have much, you are grateful for what you have. In the final years of my addiction, I felt little regard for living and had become ambivalent about being alive. But now, in recovery, I began to cherish life and develop a real sense of gratitude and a thankfulness for God, who had pulled me from the mire. It was at this time when I came to know that it was no longer my life but God's life that I was living. That's when I got a visit from Jesus.

It was the sun streaming through the window in my tiny room that first got my attention, on a seemingly routine Saturday afternoon. Everything stilled, and I became aware that something was happening. The sun, the warmth, the sense of comfort and safety, the stillness of the moment – it all felt like a divine conspiracy, and I sat spellbound at the edge of the bed. Tears welled up in my eyes and I knew they were coming from a place deep inside me – a divine place.

I felt something deep within me begin to shift. Then, as if I were being pulled by a magnetic force, I was lifted to my feet, and then pulled down onto my knees. Tears streamed down my face as I felt my heart open and course with deep love and peace and humility.

As I knelt there, I felt a physical presence next to me, shoulder to shoulder. It was Jesus. He was with me, and in his presence, I felt pure love, forgiveness and grace. I remained on my knees, sobbing. It was as if God wept through my soul, for my life. I felt as though I was being cleansed of all the pain and corruption that had afflicted me for so long. And then, there was nothing but calm.

I'm not sure how long I sat there afterward, leaning against the bed. Maybe minutes, maybe hours. I felt spent, but in a divine way. I knew that I had touched something and been touched in a way that changed me. I had always known that God was with me, but now I knew what that incarnational love felt like, and I know it still today.

✦ ✦ ✦

It was a few months before I could call my family in Idaho. I guess the hesitation was partly fear, but also because my life had been full of lies for so long, I think I wanted to get some sobriety under my belt before I could face them. I had been underground for the last two years on the streets and I would find out later that they had given me up for dead, thinking that I had found my end in some dark corner or at the hands of violence on the streets. At one point, I'd come home to an apartment I was renting in Van Nuys and found a business card from the Sheriff's Department on the door. On the back of the card was a hand-written note that said, "Your family is looking for you," and a phone number. It would be more than two more years before I would make that call.

That first call was to my sister, Peggy. I heard her shock and re-lief when she recognized my voice. Hearing hers was like coming home. We talked for a while and then she told me the news that I had suspected – my father had died, just a month before I was able to make that call. When I hung up the phone, I felt hollow and guilty. Later, my brother told me that before he died, my Dad said that he knew I was alive and that when they found me, they should tell me that he loved me.

I had waited all my life to hear him say those words. In the end he did. But by abandoning my family, I had missed it. I had ru-ined the opportunity for us to have that moment. But even then, those words meant everything to me. They still do.

Prodigal

The air was frigid and the sky gray over the cemetery. The December weather in southern Idaho can be biting cold, with temperatures ranging somewhere between zero degrees and freezing. The ground is hard. There's a peculiar absence of trees in the graveyard where my father is buried, making it seem like frozen tundra in the winter. I traveled home for the first time in more than ten years. I'd been clean and sober for eleven months, and it was also the first time I had been with my family sober since leaving Nampa twenty-five years earlier.

I was anxious about making the trip that Christmas season in 1998, nervous that my reception might be as chilly as the winter air. Over the years, my family had heard so many empty promises from me; who could blame them for thinking this was just more of the same old bullshit? I knew Peggy would welcome me – we had always been close, and her love was always truly unconditional – but my two brothers were a different story, especially my older brother, Bob. He was bitter that I had abandoned the family and wasn't there when our father died.

Don encouraged me by saying that all I had to do was show up and walk into the room sober, that my family would know because they had known me all my life. He was right. I don't think anyone doubted my sobriety. The proof was evident. I was different than they had ever seen me in my entire adult life. But that did little to assuage my brother's resentment of my disappearance over the last few years of my active addiction. All my family had good reason to feel bitter, but it was most evident with Bob. The tension was thick, and although he didn't talk with me about it, he did talk with others.

I was told about a conversation some family members had together after I had re-surfaced alive and sober. Some were complaining about my disappearing act during those later years of my addiction. At one point the talk got so heated that someone startled the others by saying *"Why don't we just kill him? Because it seems that we were much happier when we thought he was dead."* I'm told that that was a turning point in my welcome back into my family – prodigal brother, prodigal son. But it wasn't easy for Bob. I think he had always thought of himself as closest to Dad, and that indeed was probably true; he surely was a lot like my dad in many ways. He was also our father's namesake and took pride in being Bob Gibbs, Jr., so it made sense that it felt more personal for him than for others. It was also harder for him to be open to reconciliation.

So on that gray and frigid December day I found myself compelled to make the pilgrimage to my father's grave for the first time and I asked Bob to drive me there. I'm not sure why I asked him. I could have asked a number of others. Bob may have agreed out of a sense of duty; he's like that. Looking back, I feel that God was doing for us what we could not do for ourselves in that moment. On the drive out, the atmosphere inside the car didn't seem much warmer than outside. We were reserved and awkward with each other, and neither knew what to expect, so we made small talk for the thirty-minute trip through the barren frozen fields.

Bob knew right where to park. We got out of the car and stepped into the icy air. Bob took a few steps toward the graveyard, and with a nod of his head and quick point of a finger said, "It's over there." In the silent cold out in the country, the only sounds were our breathing and our feet landing on the frozen earth as we walked toward our father's grave. As we approached, Bob slowed, then stopped, and said, "Here it is." We both stood there for a moment looking at the grave marker.

ROBERT LINCOLN GIBBS
U.S. ARMY
FEBRUARY 12, 1924 – APRIL 19, 1998

Bob walked around a bit, giving me some space. My emotions were in my throat, which took me by surprise. I remembered what my brother had said about Dad insisting that I was alive when everyone else had given up, and about him leaving me that last message of love. I knew then that he had never given up on me, even though I had given up on him. It felt like those words of love had replaced the hurtful words spoken on that sidewalk outside his house all those years earlier, the words that I had carried in my bitter heart all those years. Now I remembered the goodness of the man I'd longed to know better than I ever really did. I remembered things about him – good things – that I had buried under layers of my own bitterness and self-righteousness

I knelt down on the frozen ground and for the first time in my life, talked with my father from an honest and contrite heart, the steam from my breath billowing out in bursts as I began to cry. I felt real love for my dad. With tears falling down my cheeks, I kissed the grave, hoping somehow it wasn't too late and praying that he would forgive me.

Everything went quiet in the cold winter air. The stillness was profound. It seemed like everything stopped – no sound, nothing moving – God felt close. I was on my knees on the grave, with Bob watching from a short distance. I couldn't move. I didn't want to move.

And then it happened. I felt my father's presence. It was nothing audible, just nearness, enough to let me know that he was there with me. Then silence.

I don't remember much about the ride back to town that day. But I know it was a turning point in my brother's and my relationship. There was something profound about the love of our father, expressed in death in mysterious and powerful ways, that brought us closer. Love and forgiveness is a powerful force. Bob and I have grown closer over the years, and though we are still a work in progress and we often have differing views, one thing we can embrace is that we are brothers and sons of our father.

✦ ✦ ✦

I wanted to drink and use most every day for the first year. But the one significant thing that was different this time around was that I actually began practicing a program of *recovery*. There is a big difference between "sobriety" and "recovery." If all you do is sober up a drunken horse thief, what you're left with is a sober horse thief. Putting down our drug of choice is just the tip of the iceberg. Everything that lies below the surface is where the real work of recovery begins. For some, getting down to the real causes and conditions – healing the wounds so many of us carry and becoming aware of our own character shortcomings – is deep and difficult work. But it can be done. It just takes time.

Sobriety is abstinence from mind-altering substances. Recovery is addressing the core issues that caused me to turn to those things again and again, until they eventually took my sanity and nearly my life. I think of it this way: In order to have a conscious contact with God, it is necessary to first actually be conscious – awake, with eyes wide open. My initial sobriety gave me that. The longer and deeper work of recovery that followed has allowed me to develop and nurture the conscious contact with God that is essential to any authentic life in recovery.

I was able to come to this important understanding of the nature of recovery, thanks in large part to Don's patient and loving direction. But he also held my feet to the fire. Eventually, I learned to trust that even though I was reluctant to open myself up to the truth about myself and explore the rocky terrain of my life, I would never be led down a dangerous path but instead into a way of healing.

That was new for me. Trust. Truth. Honesty. Truth sits at the center and fosters honesty and trust. These were not the standards that I had held during my life in addiction, especially those last seven years of darkness, but now they are indispensable. One thing I have come to know about the truth is that you only have one story to remember. I haven't had to change my story since the beginning of my recovery. Thank God!

This grounding in truth, supported by the spiritual principles of 12-Step recovery, set me on a path of transformation that once seemed inconceivable.

> *The great fact is this, and nothing less: That we have had deep and effective spiritual experiences which have revolutionized our whole attitude toward life, toward our fellows and toward God's universe.*
>
> —Alcoholics Anonymous

✦ ✦ ✦

Early on in my sobriety, Don encouraged me to turn myself in at the court for that old warrant I had hanging over my head – the one for having stolen plates on my car, for which I did time in County but never returned to pay the $1,000.00 fine. It was the same judge, and she wasn't happy to see me. However, she did acknowledge my willingness to place myself at the mercy of the court. I had Don with me and she seemed pleased that I was finally making a start in recovery. Then she sentenced me to three hundred hours of freeway labor as community service. It was harsh, but I knew it was fair. It was also hard work, walking behind the tree-trimming crew, dragging large branches of trees up the embankment. Before long, I was offered a seemingly easier, softer way in the form of phony papers that would show I had completed my service. I jumped at the chance to spend those Saturdays and Sundays at my leisure, in front of the air conditioner.

Remember what I said about the difference between sobriety and recovery? Well, I was sober, but surely not in recovery. If I were, I would have been practicing the principles of recovery in *all* my affairs – including my community service affairs. Instead, I still felt like the rules didn't apply to me. I was like that drunken horse thief who had gotten sober and was now nothing more than a sober horse thief. Well, the judge caught my phony papers and issued an arrest warrant. Within a couple of days, I was arrested at my new job, and when I appeared before the judge again, she was not in a good mood. She suggested I get an attorney – a good one – which I did. She stood firm on wanting to send me to prison. After a year of court appearances my lawyer got it down to six months in County Jail. I spent about half of that locked up and the rest on house arrest. I will never forget that last bid. One night in particular etched it into my memory.

I was on a floor of dorms with each housing anywhere from 50 to 100 men. One evening, just as things were beginning to quiet down for the night, a commotion began. It was in the dorm next to ours. Though we couldn't see what was happening, we could hear it clearly. At first it was hard to distinguish the sounds from any other fight breaking out, but then it became apparent that this was something different – it was the sound of a group of inmates attacking a single person. The sound of a mob. But it also became clear from the screaming that in addition to the beating, the victim was being gang-raped. His screams mingled with the sounds of the attackers shouting and encouraging each other. It was a bizarre and horrifying cacophony of brutality, sexual frenzy and agonized screams. After a while everything would go silent in a dead calm. Then it would begin again. These waves of rape and silence continued for hours through the night. We all lay on our bunks in the dorm, staring into the darkness as wave after wave of inhumane violence washed over us. Some covered their heads with pillows.

It was soul-shattering. It was evil. Where the hell was God? Why didn't God stop this? The answers to those questions would eventually come, but not this night.

The next morning, we watched as the deputies and medical staff removed the young man from the neighboring dorm. The sight was horrifying. He was unrecognizable. His face was swollen and disfigured, bloodied and black and blue. It made me sick. I had to turn away. It also reminded me of another night I had witnessed the violence that people are capable of – the night my stepfather Elmer burst through our front door and opened fire in a drunken frenzy of jealous rage. I knew that night in the dark dungeon of this jail, like that night in our blood-spattered living room in Idaho all those years earlier, would not soon – if ever – be forgotten.

I did a couple more months after that night before being released on house arrest. That brief period was a real turning point for me. All of the dehumanizing and violence was the same; the only thing different was that I was sober, albeit still a horse thief.

Like that New Year's Eve morning, staggering out of the van beaten and bloodied, this was another moment of clarity that if something didn't change, nothing would truly change for me.

That was when I first learned – the hard way – the difference between being sober and being in recovery. There are many opportunities to drink or get high in jail, but this time, something had shifted in me. After I was released, I decided to pour myself into real recovery – going to meetings, working the program, engaging in the fellowship, working with other alcoholics and doing the 12-Step work with Don. I never looked back again, and that understanding of the true nature of recovery versus mere sobriety has completely transformed my life. I started taking A.A. panels into institutions – mostly hospitals and in-patient treatment centers. That's what planted the seed of a primary purpose in my life: to stay sober and to help others.

Spiritually sick, like me

Making that start in recovery meant dealing with thorny issues like shame, anger, resentment and dishonesty. I had to face some hard truths about myself: how I had hurt others and how I was to blame for almost all of my troubles – not those I had been pointing the finger at all those years. Like a lot of others, I had bad things happen to me, but no one forced my mouth open and poured drinks down my throat. *I* did that. I wasn't just a victim of my circumstances, but a willing participant, at least in the beginning. But for me, like many alcoholics, there came a time when I no longer had the power of choice. At that point, I slipped over the edge and lost the ability to choose for myself, and then the monster of addiction took total control. It's a sinister and frightening reality.

This doesn't mean that some of the resentments we hold

toward others who have harmed us are invalid. The extreme physical abuse at the hands of my stepfather and stepmother was very real and harmful. The abandonment by my mother and the emotional absence of my father caused deep wounds as well. Circumstances like these surely contributed to the sense of low self-esteem, shame and sense of unworthiness that fueled my addiction and they were not of my making. But I have learned that although I may not be responsible for those things, I *am* responsible for my recovery. Once you know this kind of truth, you can never not know it again. Now that I am aware of the truth about myself and the spiritual tools at my disposal, the success or failure of my recovery rests squarely on my shoulders and nowhere else.

I spent much of my life pointing the finger at people I blamed for all my problems. Elmer was at the top of the list. How could I ever be free of my anger toward the man who beat us regularly and opened fire that night in a drunken murderous rage? It seemed impossible, and maybe it was for me, but not for God. But how could I truly see Elmer as God sees him? It might be easier for me to see others that way, but not Elmer.

There is something that sits in the center of the Twelve Steps that changed my life. These words are at the center of the personal inventory process: "*This was our course: we realized that the people who wronged us were perhaps spiritually sick. Though we did not like their symptoms and the way these disturbed us, they like ourselves, were sick too.*" Those few words were then, and are still to this day, a huge game-changer for me. They level the playing field. The words presented an instant paradox. On one hand, I couldn't imagine feeling that generous and compassionate about people like my step-father. On the other hand, I knew deep down that there was profound truth in these words – truth that could lead me to freedom. That is exactly what has happened. The deep resentment I once held has been taken away, making room for compassion. Yes, that's right – compassion instead of hatred.

One day after about twenty years in recovery, during a community gathering at the monastery, someone asked me to get a certain photo they had seen before that they thought was interesting. I went to my monk's cell and opened a suitcase containing my keepsakes and old photos. As I was flipping through the photos, out fell one taken some fifty years earlier. It was a picture of Elmer sitting drunk in a bar. The shock in seeing it took my breath away momentarily, but then quickly became a response of compassion. In that photo I could see the lost soul, the tragic life. Sitting there in my monastery cell holding that image, I prayed for Elmer – for his peace. I knew that he was indeed in peace, because I knew he was in the arms of God. That day I saw Elmer as God saw him: with compassion. This is the miracle of recovery. This is the fruit of choosing the narrow gate that leads to life.

I truly believe that a number of things have to come together at just the right time in order for us to make a new start. For me, I needed to be as desperate as I was – as only the dying can be – to allow for that critical willingness to step in the right direction. I feel that the right people need to be in the right place at the right time – people like Don and Lawrence – who caught me at just the right moment and gave me a safe and soft place to land as well as some good honest advice. The awareness that someone actually cared enough to help me was huge. Of course, God's grace is in the mix, grace that creates just enough opening for the sunlight of the Spirit. All these things and more come together in a flash – in a nanosecond – and we are allowed to slip through to the other side and get sober. All those things happened for me, and today when I speak at A.A. meetings, I often say that all those things have happened for everyone in the room. I don't know if I would ever have another chance of those things coming together in that way again, and I'm not willing to take the chance. Besides, my life today is second to none. I am truly living a life of happiness, joy and freedom. It hasn't always been easy, but it has been worth every minute.

Conscious contact

After a couple of years in real recovery – meaning that I was truly working the program, which included admitting to my innermost self that I was an alcoholic and a drug addict, knowing that I had to turn to a power greater than myself for help, doing the tough work of self-examination in getting to the root of my problem and making amends to those I had harmed – I had arrived at Step Eleven, which encourages us to seek through prayer and meditation a conscious contact with God. This was something I not only knew I needed, but was also eager and excited to find. I have always had that thing inside me – that knowing of God that my grandmother had instilled when I was just a boy – so this felt like I was tuning into the homing device that had always been quietly and patiently pulsing within me.

I started looking for a faith community to connect with. Initially that meant the Catholic faith that I had been baptized into some ten years earlier. But I was on different footing now. I was grounded in my recovery and more aware of myself than ever before. I quickly found that Catholicism was not the right fit. I respected the tradition and sacraments, and I loved the mystical nature of it all, but I needed a church community that I felt was more open to my views on women's leadership, open Communion, and human sexuality. Don and I had many conversations, and eventually he pointed me to another friend in recovery who attended the Episcopal Church. It didn't take long before I knew I was home there. It had all the right elements: women priests, open Communion and an understanding that all people were equally loved and cherished by God. Period. No exceptions. Coming from the rough-and-tumble life I had led, I was welcomed with open arms and told not only was I beloved, but also that the life I had led, and the lessons learned from that life, were a gift to the Church.

My regular attendance in church soon led to my interest in contemplative spirituality. I started practicing Centering Prayer and *Lectio Divina* to enrich my already consistent prayer life, and this began taking me deeper into my relationship with God and opening new vistas in relationships with others. A real turning point for me came in 2003 when Doyt, a friend and priest at All Saints Church in Beverly Hills, invited me to a retreat at the Mount Calvary Monastery in Santa Barbara overlooking the Pacific Ocean. Mount Calvary was one of five monasteries of the Order of the Holy Cross, one of the oldest Episcopal monastic orders in the United States. The Santa Barbara location was an old Spanish-style villa that had been converted to a monastery some sixty years earlier. From its mountaintop location, the views were breathtaking.

It was the first time I had ever experienced a monastic community. I loved everything about it – the silence, community, chanting, bells and the rich intentionality of it all. I will never forget that first visit. Once again, I had the feeling that I was home.

One afternoon, while Doyt and I were sitting in one of the small libraries together, he began to talk about what he had witnessed in the progression of my spiritual life over the previous two years. Then he looked at me and asked, "Have you ever considered the monastic life?" The question penetrated me. After I said no, he said, "Maybe you should." We talked about what that might look like and mean for my life. That day in the monastery overlooking the Pacific Ocean, the seed was planted.

Carrying the message

In 2004, with six years of recovery under my belt, I began to volunteer with my friends in the jails. At first, working with the incarcerated was an unsettling consideration, but I was somehow brave enough to follow God's desire for me. I started volunteering one Sunday each month, helping with church services in jail facilities. That led to adding a Friday night, and on and on until eventually, with the support of our bishop and others, I was able to quit my sales job and dedicate myself completely to the jail ministry. I had considered Doyt's question about a monastic vocation, and was in spiritual direction with Brother Robert at Mount Calvary Monastery discerning my call as a monk. But I had already begun jail ministry and couldn't see myself leaving it. Part of me was conflicted and even disappointed that the monastic life didn't seem to be on the cards.

In 2005 I met with Carol, the rector of our parish. As an associate at Mount Calvary, I had had been praying the Divine Office in a small corner of my apartment twice each day – morning and evening – asking God to show me the way forward. After a few months the answer became clear: be ordained as clergy in the church. I made the appointment with Carol. I walked in and said that God had told me that I was to be ordained as a deacon in the church. Her response was immediate. "Fantastic!" she said. "Let's put together a discernment committee and get things going."

On May 23, 2010, the Day of Pentecost, after four years of

seminary studies and all the formation required of clergy in the Episcopal Church, Bishop Chet Talton ordained me to the Sacred Order of Deacons.

Photo: David Palmer - David Palmer Images, 2010

✦ ✦ ✦

My primary ministry was (and remains) jail ministry. The Episcopal presence in the jails began growing. In June of that year, I requested – and was granted – our own religious program designation. The formal establishment of the Episcopal Church in the jails was a real game-changer, and would have long-term and lasting effect. There now will always be a place for the Episcopal Church in the L.A. County Jails.

Something else happened during that time. In 2008, I met Greta Ronningen, who was new to Los Angeles and aspiring to chaplaincy. Greta was living a rule of life as a fellow with the Society of Saint John the Evangelist (SSJE) in Cambridge, Massachusetts, much like my own living of the rule as an associate of Holy Cross. She came to a talk I was giving and immediately embraced the idea of ministry with the incarcerated, which now had evolved into PRISM Restorative Justice, a growing ministry of the Episcopal Diocese of Los Angeles. Greta brought an energy and commitment to the ministry at just the right time, and PRISM would not be what it is today without Sister Greta.

At one point, Greta and I were visiting SSJE and her spiritual father, Brother Eldridge Pendleton. It was during that visit that we first became aware of the prompting to begin our own religious community grounded in our love for the monastic way of life and our ministry in the jails. We enlisted the wisdom of our spiritual directors, monks from both Mount Calvary and SSJE, as well as our bishops. After several months, the consensus by all was that this was an authentic call from God. After a year of formation under the mentorship of The Order of Holy Cross (Mount Calvary) and the guidance and loving care of Brother Nicholas Radelmiller, we were clothed as monastic novices, thus establishing the Community of Divine Love at First Vespers of the Feast of All Saints in 2010. We opened our new monastery location in San Gabriel, California that same year. Today, Community of Divine Love continues to flourish both in our contemplative prayer life in the monastery enclosure as well as in our ministry in the jails. We are deeply grateful to Brother Nick and Brother Eldridge for their wisdom and loving support. May their souls rest in peace, knowing the good work they began with us continues.

Contemplation and action

Inside the jails, we are immersed in deep suffering and the complexities of the human condition of those we are companions with in exile. To remain grounded, it is essential to have a contemplative community as a place to return to. That's what the monastery enclosure of Community of Divine Love is for us. Our monastic experience there has emerged as both contemplative and active. Our life in the monastery enclosure informs everything we do outside it, particularly in the jails. Our silence, prayer (we pray as a community four times each day), study, contemplative practices, meditation and work around the monastery all contribute to how we live and move and have our being in the facilities of mass incarceration. But we are aware that those men and women living life locked up are also our teachers, from whom we have much to learn. This is what I call the holy exchange of gifts.

In entering the monastic life, we were encouraged by our desire for the love and mercy of God. It is a life that renounces and pro- tests against the things of the world that would distract us from that love. We live a vow of poverty that protests the materialism of the world. We live a vow of celibacy that levels the playing field of relationship with others, and frees us to welcome all people with equal decency, honesty and love. We live a vow of obedi- ence to God's will in our lives in whatever way it is authentically expressed. In our community, we also live a vow of stability that commits to staying in this place, come what may. External sta- bility fosters internal stability in a sometimes-shifting world. We also live a vow of conversion of life that challenges us to be aware that God is always calling us to new places with newness and freshness of life. All of these elements of the monastic life in our community help us to engage with the world with clean hearts and spirits that are open, loving and truthful. In this way we are free to become all that God desires us to be. That is also what we want for all of our friends, whether they are locked up or free.

Photo: Chris Tumilty

Photo: Greta Ronningen

Wasted

Twenty-five years
wasted
drunk
loaded
wired
in the end
spent
done in and tired out
withered and ravaged
wasted
but not worthless
futile
but not fruitless
for out of the land of oblivion
comes wisdom
by grace
no longer wasted
sitting in this Divine Saloon
staggering drunk
intoxicated
with God.   —Brother Dennis

CHAPTER EIGHT

Holy · Holy · Holy

There is nothing quite like the experience of a church service behind bars.

I have been fortunate to worship God in small communities and in larger gatherings; in simple chapels, large cathedrals and beautiful monasteries; on noisy city streets and in the quiet stillness of nature; in places all across the United States and Canada; on the shores of Galilee, in Jerusalem, Mexico and Haiti. I have held hands with 75,000 others at a world recovery convention at the Toronto Sky Dome, reciting the Lord's Prayer together.

These experiences have been beautiful and powerful. And yet nothing can compare to breaking bread and being on my knees on the concrete with my brothers and sisters in the jails. The deep reverence, the real awareness of the need for mercy and desire for amendment of life, is real and palpable here. There is also another layer to all of this that is incredible: many of those worshipping God during incarceration have a genuine and deep sense of gratitude for what God is doing in their lives. Even in the hard struggle of life in jail, these holy men and women praise God. Witnessing this kind of faith and love for God while walking the hard road is amazing and something I wish that every person could experience at least once. It will change you in ways you might never know otherwise – I know it has changed me, and continues to change me every single day. This is sacred space where hearts are transformed by our love of God, by God's love for us and by our love for each other. This truly is holy ground.

✦   ✦   ✦

I press the play button to start gathering music for our church service on the 5000 Floor of Men's Central Jail. I always try to choose something with energy, something to get the spirit moving in the room and help everyone shift gears from their life in cells or dorms to an experience of worship. Sometimes it's more modern praise and worship music, but I often open things up a bit with a wider, more diverse music mix like reggae, traditional spirituals or monastic chanting. Today it's the sound of George Harrison's "My Sweet Lord" pulsing through the large chapel. As about forty men start to enter the space we start clapping to the beat and before I know it, everyone is keeping near-perfect time. Some are standing and swaying, some start to pick up on the chorus:

My sweet Lord,
I really want to know you,
I really want to show you Lord,
But it takes so long, my Lord …

Man, the place is jumpin'. The energy of the room has changed.

Our collective hearts seem to be beating as one. This is sacred space. For a moment we might even have forgotten that we are in jail.

This group of men is from the PC dorms, meaning protective custody, mainly because they either have a credible threat on their life or they are considered at high risk to be targeted for harm in general population. As a result, they get very little programming (services such as church, groups, A.A. meetings, and so on). We are not even allowed to pull them out to a place for individual spiritual care. We do our best to have intimate conversations, but it is never private. These are suffocating circumstances, where it seems that those who need the most get the very least.

It feels like God's grace that we were somehow able to arrange with the Sheriff's Department to hold this once-per-week church service on Thursday afternoons. In order to make it work, the entire floor of the jail, consisting of eight dorms and hundreds of men, is completely locked down to allow our friends to be escorted to the chapel for the service. So now they come, on their weekly sojourn from exile, to this space. It might be the closest thing there is to the Promised Land in this wasteland of a jail. We try to make the most of it. The air of the large chapel is misted with aromatherapy oils. We come prepared with lots of magazines, pencils, daily devotionals, and a various assortment of things, all for the taking. Rosaries are a big hit and so is the music.

"My Sweet Lord" begins to fade, but the energy is still moving. The environment has changed. No longer a large empty, bland room, it has been infused by the Spirit and anointed by the presence of these holy men. Riding the wave of that energy, I ask a question most are used to hearing: "Who can name that artist?" There are no takers. Most of the men are too young to know about the music of the 70s or 80s. So I tell them it's George Harrison, and that he was a deeply spiritual man and a member of the Beatles.

This gets some takers. "Oh yeah, the Beatles. This guy was one of them?" one guy asks. Another guy shouts out, "I don't know about any Beatles, but that guy is BADASS!" Another asks, what were all the other words he was chanting at the end? I explain that they were taken from the Hindu tradition and some were from Sanskrit, one of the oldest known languages in the world, and that they were names for God as the people of that tradition understand God. Music can be a teacher.

We settle down a bit, and I run through a couple of guidelines for the worship for anyone new. Then, as always, before we begin we hold a moment of complete silence to be aware of God's presence among us. It's a quietly powerful moment. The energy of the Spirit has shifted again. After a full minute or so, we are ready to begin.

I always have several of the men help lead the worship, and they are right up front behind the improvised altar. Each leader has a part. Today Manuel is reading the Epistle; Jason, the Gospel; Enrique is leading the psalm. Thomas, who is new today, leads the Prayers of the People. Some of the others will share parts of the Eucharistic Prayer. If someone is fumbling with his part, the others always kindly help him along. In those moments I see their sweetness. I often have one of the men serve the bread while I offer an anointing. This feels like real community, the way Jesus imagined it for us. It's beautiful because the men are beautiful, and it's powerful because it's so real. There really is nothing that compares.

During Holy Communion, I queue up "Angel" by Sarah McLachlan. It continues for some time after everyone has received the bread and the anointing. Men are on their knees praying, weeping and connecting with something deep within yet beyond ourselves. I'm weeping as I sit with the men around the altar as the music ends. We sit in silence, allowing ourselves to be held by the Mystery of Love in the moment, and by one another. Finally, I stand and move to the altar for the concluding prayer. I can tell even the deputies standing watch at the door are taken in by the moment.

After the service, Thomas, who led the group in prayer earlier, sits quietly. He asks if we can talk. I sit and listen as he tells me about how a couple of weeks earlier, he was released from the jail by mistake. Although the mistake was discovered and he was re-arrested about a week later, he was able to visit his dying mother during those few days of freedom. As he spoke, he dropped a single tear, then began sobbing. His mother Robin, had died two days earlier. Through his tears he thanked God for the "mistake" that set him free so he could see his mother. He knows it was no mere mistake, and I know it too. It was God's grace. It's no wonder that we call it amazing.

This is worship in Men's Central Jail.

✦　✦　✦

I walk onto the housing floor in Men's Central Jail and in one of the dorms I see an 8" x 11" white paper sign with big bold black print that says: **THIS IS HOLY GROUND.** It has been posted on the wall near someone's bunk. It's not the only one. We have been handing out these signs for years, and they are popular with those who are trying to reimagine their environment. It's a different way of tagging – marking your territory for God. They help to remind us that even within the struggle and darkness of this place, God's light shines and this remains holy ground. Sometimes places feel holy because something big happened there. Others feel holy because so many people have come to the place to pray and the energy of all of those prayerful souls have made it holy.

When I visited the holy land of Israel in 2007 I remember standing in places where something big had supposedly happened – you know, a big moment in biblical history – and the funny thing was that I didn't always "feel it." I would think, "Shouldn't I be feeling something here?" And then there were other moments when I would be in a seemingly run-of-the-mill place and be taken by surprise and completely captured by the holiness of the place. What I know now is that if a place feels holy, it *is* holy. The jail is such a place.

✦ ✦ ✦

Holy Tears

One of the most intimate and memorable moments of worship I have known came in a seemingly unlikely place, although I have come to expect such things from God.

The place was the dayroom on the psychiatric floor of the clinic in Twin Towers Correctional Facility. Twin Towers houses about 4,000 inmates, both male and female, all of whom are diagnosed with varying degrees of psychological challenges. It is the largest mental health facility in the United States, and it's a jail. This is clear and alarming evidence that we are incarcerating our mentally ill in numbers we have never seen before. It both saddens and disturbs me that because of our failing as a society to properly deal with issues such as mental illness, we instead just throw people in jail. But using incarceration as an answer to our mental health care challenge doesn't make people's problems go away. As Angela Davis said some forty years ago, the only thing that disappears is the human being.

I have met thousands of these "invisible" people. And by *invisible*, I mean people who are tucked away in jails and institutions, hidden from the mainstream view. But I am here to say that there are no throwaway people. There are only people who, regardless of who they are or what they may or may not have done, are held in God's grace and love as God's beloved children. Chavez is one such person.

Chavez speaks only broken English. She was deeply fractured from the tragic and traumatic events that had landed her in jail. She would come to my small intimate gathering for worship in the psych unit on the fourth floor of the clinic each Tuesday morning with four or five others, shuffling into the small recreation room draped in dark blue "suicide gowns" fashioned out of the same material used for furniture pads and fastened only with Velcro strips. It's bizarre that they refer to these as gowns. They are terribly degrading and yet, oddly, the women seem to somehow transcend the degradation with grace, in a way that helps me to not see the gown, but only the person. Of those who would attend, Chavez was the one who, while never saying anything, always helped me set the altar, which was a three-foot-square table. Together, we would spread the white altar covering, liturgical colored band and fair linen. She always did it with such gentle intention and reverence. She loved placing the cross and she always sat directly across from me, with just the width of the table separating us. She would fix her gentle gaze upon that cross during Eucharist.

Once, while we were taking a quiet moment of reflection, as we always did after sharing Communion, I opened my eyes to

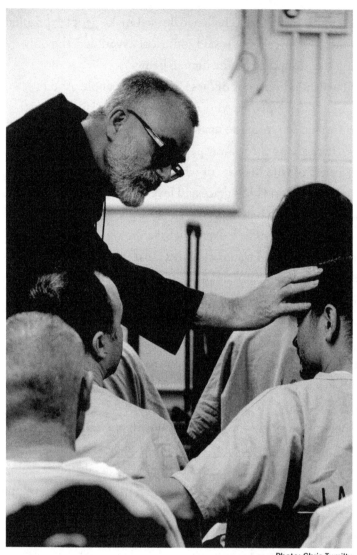

Photo: Chris Tumilty

the sight of the white fair linen. Suddenly and silently I saw her teardrop land. I heard Chavez whisper, "Thank you, Jesus." I knew that God's tears were mingling with her own in that moment. God's grace was with her pain and her comfort.

This is a place where the awareness of one's need of God's healing is very real. It is also a place where the experience of that grace is very real. And there are moments when this divine grace cuts through all of the complexities of life here, and we are allowed to experience the stunning and breathtaking reality of God's love up close.

✦ ✦ ✦

God's Tears

I saw God's tears today
falling from your eyes
mingling with God's own
springing from love
and sadness within
the source the soul
where living waters flow
God's tears
our tears
one heart
one love   —Brother Dennis

Holy Water

On a Sunday, while one of our chaplains was setting things up for church services on one of the housing modules, the control booth announced over the loudspeaker: "EPISCOPAL CHURCH SERVICES! IF YOU WANT TO ATTEND EPISCOPAL SERVICES, LINE UP AT THE POD DOOR."

One of the inmates was heard yelling out across the pods,

"What kind of services?" Another inmate yelled back: "It's EPIS-COPAL – you know, the one where everyone is welcome."

Never before or since have I experienced the Episcopal Church's slogan – The Episcopal Church Welcomes You – come to life in such a way in real time, and it says a lot about how our chaplains and programs are perceived in the jails. In a world that all too often seems to want to divide us, our message is clear: We are equally loved by God – all of us – and we are here to experience and foster that love in community.

Those living in exile in jail, like many others in the world, have a deep longing for such truth. Jesus called them "the least of these who are my family," and the last thing they need is to be pushed outside the circle. What they do need – what we all need – is love. None of us are without our own shortcomings, but no matter who we are or what we have done, no one is beyond God's grace and love. Our task is to be instruments of that love for one another. Final judgment is God's work; ours is something different. The people we walk with in the jails long for this kind of redemptive love. They, like all of us, are thirsty for the clear water from the cup of salvation. This is the water that we share with each other.

> Let anyone who is thirsty come to me and drink. Whoever believes in me, as Scripture has said, rivers of living water will flow from within them. —John 7:37-38

Baptisms have become increasingly common for us. I'm sure it has something to do with our unconditional and all-inclusive presence in the jails. For some inmates, it is the first time in life that they have found a spiritual community that welcomes all people as they are. For others, it might be that they feel safe to reclaim who they are and free to rediscover their faith. Quite often, people are drawn to the baptismal waters because they have come to realize that the transformation they experience stems from living our common life together based on the spiritual principles of the life and teachings of Jesus. Whatever it is that brings people to this important moment, it is a joyful day, and I am quite sure that all the company of heaven rejoices when they find their footing on the path from brokenness to healing and wholeness.

✦   ✦   ✦

Ricky, when I first met him, was about as tough as they come around here. I used to good-naturedly refer to him as a "cowboy," which he accepted with easy pride. He's an intimidating young man. He's strong and cocky, and he has the scars to prove that he's been through more than a few rough rides. He once told me that he never felt more powerful than when he had a bag of dope in his pocket and a gun in his waistband. But he's worked hard to change.

Like him, a lot of men have been hardened by the life, but if you stay with them – I mean really stay with them – you will see the sweetness. You will see the little boy in them. Like most of the men I spend time with, Ricky has been one of my teachers as I have watched his heart of stone soften. I have seen him struggle to turn away from the violence that he has known so well in his life. I have also heard about it when he was in the "hole" (solitary confinement) again for reverting to that violence and swinging on someone. The fights are often about people feeling as if they have been disrespected – little things that can lead to big trouble. It may start with someone looking at them the wrong way, or bumping into them, or saying something, and in a flash of a few seconds, it's on. These kinds of toxic reactions most likely come from deep wounds that have never been tended and healed. Most of the men in jail have their own versions of these deep wounds. They have just never been taught how to heal them.

This day, the altar was set with fair linen again, this time in a small dayroom located at the end of the row where Ricky was living. Four of us gathered to share this holy experience of baptism. Another table, cleaned with paper towels and water, was dressed for the occasion in gold and white. The sterling silver ciborium (a small box holding the consecrated bread that represents the Body of Christ) and lavabo (water bowl) glistened in the otherwise drab environment. It was as though a divine light shone on that makeshift altar and the entire space was illumined with it. We began the Holy Eucharist amidst the noise and chaos of the row, where forty other men carried on with their lives and yelled back and forth from the upper and lower tiers. But in this holy moment, even the cacophony of noise sounded sacred. It was if all of the life of those rows was joining in the chorus of angels.

Once again, the holy water flowed. It flowed from the silver lavabo over Ricky's head, and it flowed from our eyes. Once again, the awareness of the soul's need for healing was met by divine grace, and streams of living water flowed through our collective heart. I couldn't help but notice a tiny spot of water that had once again found a resting place on the linen. I remembered Chavez and was reminded that we are all connected in mysterious and wonderful ways.

✦ ✦ ✦

I still remember my own baptism. That Easter Vigil evening in 1989 I was baptized in the name of the Father, the Son, and the Holy Spirit, sealed by the Holy Spirit in baptism and marked as Christ's own forever. I truly felt that the Holy Spirit of God touched me in a way like I had never known before. Something important had happened in that moment, but it was only in the years that followed that I would come to more fully understand and to embrace the full import of what the sacrament of baptism means. The experience continues to unfold even today.

I think that is how it often is for many of us. We make a decision, we bring ourselves – imperfect as we are – to the waters of baptism, and then the process of realizing what the deeper meaning of it all begins to unfold. As the Buddhists say, the path is made by walking. I know for sure that even though I may not have fully understood the impact my baptism would have on my life, the Holy Spirit was working with me.

I love Luke's telling of Jesus' baptism and how he was with all the others at the Jordan River that day. Jesus' public baptism was an act of solidarity with *all people*. He simply got in line with all the others whose lives may have been broken and who were turning to God with hopes for a new beginning and a new life. Jesus aligned himself with all people. He identified with the downtrodden and the marginalized. His baptism was, and is, in solidarity with those being baptized in churches, rivers, lakes, hospitals and jails.

> *Living water shall flow from Jerusalem*
> *and the Lord shall be King over the whole earth!*
> *The waters of a river give joy to the city of God.*
> —Sprinkling Rite
> Lauds and Vespers
> Camaldolese Monks, OSB

During my 2007 pilgrimage to the Holy Land, when we visited the Jordan River I couldn't help but remember that Easter Vigil night so many years before at Saint Francis' Church. I thought of how I had come for healing, as a way to turn my life around, crying out to God the only way I knew how: through the waters of baptism. At the time I didn't fully realize what it would all mean for me. But God knew, and that's all that mattered.

Kneeling on the bank of the Jordan River, I remembered that I had indeed been cleansed in baptism all those years ago, and it has been the *experience* of the kingdom-life in the years that followed that has allowed the healing power of God's grace to change my life. As I dipped my head into the River Jordan, I remembered that I had been sealed by the Holy Spirit in baptism and marked as Christ's own forever. It is also my covenant with God that has brought me to walk in solidarity with my incarcerated sisters and brothers. In the Episcopal tradition, we make baptismal commitment that we will seek and serve Christ in all persons, loving our neighbors as ourselves; strive for justice and peace among all people; and respect the dignity of every human being.

At our monastery, we have a holy water font centrally located in the chapel. Several times a day, as we come and go from praying the Divine Offices together, we touch that water, we touch our foreheads and our hearts and we remember who we are as monks. And each time we do, we are affirming the centrality of Christ in our lives and our commitment to live as followers of Jesus, our Lord.

✦ ✦ ✦

The 9000 floor of Men's Central Jail is where our gay and transgendered brothers and sisters live during incarceration. The floor consists of five large dorms, each housing between 75 and 150 people. I have been working closely with this community since 2015. On Sundays we worship together, and on Wednesdays we walk our common path of transformation together in Sacred Journey Listening Circles. I also spend countless hours in individual conversations about our life together. This is the extreme edge of life in exile. And it is here that I first met Tommy.

Tommy's is a story of real transformation and an example of what God can do given an open and willing heart to work with. I first met Tommy when he started attending the Sacred Journey, and right from the beginning, I could sense that he was seeking more than just a break from the drama of jail dorm life, although that is how some find their way to our programs or worship services. The incarcerated life is filled with chaos, constant loud chatter, high-volume televisions usually set to such cultural programming gems as Jerry Springer, deputies calling out directives from the loud speaker system and slamming of heavy metal doors. The noise is constant and relentless. So really, who could blame anyone for using church or a spiritual formation class as an opportunity to escape the madhouse of the dorms?

I often feel that if nothing else is accomplished during our time together, at least the men and women have had a break from it all and found a centering place. They find clear water, they drink and they come back for more. Tommy had an attentiveness and focus that told me he was truly seeking something. And so there he was, every Sunday for church and every Wednesday for the Sacred Journey. Like many we encounter, he had never met a monk before and was curious about our life. Over time, Tommy took a keen interest in the study of Benedictine spirituality and how it might help him finish his time in a more fulfilling way. He began to have his partner order books and have them shipped directly to the jail. During the last year of his state prison term, Tommy read more books on Benedictine spirituality than I had read in my nearly ten years of monastic life. In fact, Tommy would finish a book and then give it to me to read; a couple of these have become required reading for our monastery. It's clear evidence that we are all teachers and we are all students.

This speaks to our understanding of *Monks Behind Bars*, which is our philosophy that we are indeed monks walking with our incarcerated friends behind bars. We also hope to help others become monks behind bars in their spiritual formation while locked up. Tommy is a good example of this.

After about a year of Christian formation, Tommy was baptized in the Episcopal Church on Easter Day 2016. It was a deeply moving experience, with those who had walked with Tommy along the sometimes-hard road of reconciliation and redemption standing in witness as the water once again poured and landed on that fair linen.

✦ ✦ ✦

I got the call on a Friday. We were getting things ready for Holy Eucharist following breakfast at the monastery, which had been preceded by praying Lauds (a monastic prayer service) that morning. It was a pretty typical Friday morning at the monastery.

That is, until my phone rang. It was Sergeant Martinez from the L.A. County Sheriff's Department's Office of Religious and Volunteer Services. There had been an accident involving one of the inmate firefighters who was part of the crew responding to a wildfire in Malibu. The only information was that the inmate firefighter had life-threatening injuries and was being helicoptered to UCLA Medical Center. Sgt. Martinez asked me to come immediately. Our relationship over the years had become such that our chaplain programs were now the first to get such calls from ORVS. I was then whisked by sheriff's escort to the hospital to be with the inmate and her family.

As I arrived I learned that Shawna, the inmate firefighter, had been hit in the head by a boulder falling down the mountain. Part of her skull had been crushed, and she was on life support, with no real hope for survival. I stood in the room with Shawna as the doctors and nursing staff reviewed the latest information with me. She was so young, only twenty-two. Her mother had just arrived at the hospital and was in the waiting area outside the Intensive Care Unit. She had already been told of Shawna's prognosis. I looked at the family – sisters, cousins, aunts, uncles – through the small glass window. It was all very sad and tragic. The nurse pointed out Diana, Shawna's mother, to me.

My heart was sinking and anxious at the same time. I took a deep breath, braced myself, and pushed the door open. They all turned to look in my direction. I was aware of what I often notice when wearing clericals in public: some people look at me with welcoming relief, others with suspicion or avoidance. I went first to Diana and introduced myself as a chaplain. She was glad to see me, and we stepped apart to talk. It wasn't long before she was sobbing. All I could do was hold her. This mother's grief for her young daughter is something I will never forget. It drew me into the depths of the something I could not and may never fully understand.

It came time for us to go into Shawna's room. It was just the three of us – Shawna, Diana, and me – and nurses coming in to tend to Shawna. Diana and I sat on each side of Shawna's bed. Diana held her daughter's left hand. I held her right. Diana told me stories about Shawna and their years together. Life hadn't been easy for any of them. This time was sacred, deeply saddening and tragic. Diana mentioned that just two weeks before, Shawna had talked about continuing on the good track she had begun while locked up. She had talked about being baptized. Diana looked at me and said, "Is it too late?" I assured her that it was not. I opened my Book of Common Prayer to page 299, *Holy Baptism*. We read the story of Jesus' own baptism. We prayed and we poured holy water and we touched Shawna with holy chrism oil. We baptized her in the name of the Father, the Son and the Holy Spirit. We marked her as Christ's own forever and sealed her with the Holy Spirit. Once again the holy water flowed – from God and from our eyes. And this time it fell on the white bed linens where Shawna lay. It felt like our altar in that room. It felt holy, and it was holy.

Over the next twenty-four hours I sat with Shawna for hours at a time, just the two of us. Though she couldn't speak, I am absolutely certain that she heard my whispered words, my quiet prayers. I am just as certain of my awareness of the energy between us. I know that I will never forget the special connection that was and continues to be shared between us. I stayed with her late into the night of the second day, until the time came to remove her life support – her last tether to this world.

It was just the two of us – a young woman and her chaplain – and we said goodbye.

That Thursday, forty members of her female inmate fire-fighting crew stood in honor of their fallen sister during a memorial service at the Malibu Fire Camp. Two days later I joined the procession that escorted Shawna the sixty miles back to her hometown of Lancaster to be with her family and friends. All along the journey, whenever we came to a freeway overpass, we saw fellow firefighters from all jurisdictions, lining the overpasses with their fire trucks, in full-dress uniform and standing at attention, saluting Shawna – their fallen comrade – as she passed by. This is what God's kingdom is like, with all the company of heaven praising and honoring Shawna as one of God's beloved children, welcoming her into God's heavenly kingdom.

I was asked to offer the eulogy at Shawna's memorial service. It was big and public, with hundreds of people in attendance, including law enforcement and fire department personnel. But I will never forget those quiet long hours together alone in that hospital room. I will never forget touching her with the holy water of baptism and anointing her for her journey with God. That night, our paths had crossed in a divine moment in time. Times like these are so intimate, so sacred and so affecting that one's life is never the same afterward. This was such a moment, and it came together in tragedy and grace through the holy waters of baptism.

✦ ✦ ✦

I know that all the company of heaven rejoices when anyone, anywhere choses God for their life. But there is something that feels especially deep and affecting about these baptisms that come about during the time of exile in prison. We see it during Eucharist when men and women are on their knees and tears are flooding their face in a moment of compunction and grace. We see it in lives being transformed in real time before our very eyes. We see it in the contriteness of heart and the real *metanoia* – the deep turning to God – that has happened in ways that it may not have happened elsewhere. We see it in the real humility, grace and generosity of these men and women that is the fruit of salvation. Yes, this is holy ground. These are holy tears. This is where holy water flows.

The yearning to know about God and how God is working in the lives of our incarcerated friends is real, and the desire to see God in their circumstances is authentic. Sometimes we hear the question, "Why did God put me in jail?" "Do you think God put me here for a reason – to teach me a lesson?" These are good questions and opportunities to open things up a bit in our understanding of the nature of God. My responses are typically something like: No, I don't believe God puts anyone in prison. I think people put people in prison. Sometimes people put themselves in prison (that's always a conversation opener!). I don't feel that the compassionate God of love that I know would want these terrible conditions for anyone. What I *do* feel is that free will can land us in this place of exile, either our own free will in making bad choices, or – in the case of those who are falsely accused and truly innocent – the free will of another human being (that is, the abuse of one's free will). In either case, when we are stuck behind bars, it seems that God will use the opportunity to work with us, now that he has our full attention.

People often ask me if I feel we are "effective" in our ministry in the jails. They wonder if what we do makes a difference. It's a hard question to answer. The truth is, I wonder that same thing myself sometimes. Maybe my best and most honest answer is that I don't know if we are changing anyone or, for that matter, making a difference in the world, but I know *my* world is continuously transformed. The awareness of the grace of God reveals itself regularly in sometimes surprising, but always breathtaking ways in this place. I see God's tears mingling with those of humans and falling down their faces as they hold out their hands to receive the Body of Christ – the Bread of Life. And sometimes the hands reaching for hope in Communion are those of a person wearing a deputy sheriff's uniform, standing in the same space with those in jail blues. I see knees on the concrete floor in real and deep prayer. I see real joy and eagerness for the things of God. I see grace and I see love.

Many men and women say that they have never felt closer to God than when they were in jail. They talk about the nearness of our Creator being real for them in this time of struggle and darkness. I see men and women truly giving themselves to the work of spiritual growth. Some people talk about "jailhouse conversion" in a way that diminishes the authenticity of the experience. The cynical may say that these people are seeking God only because their backs are against the wall and they have no other way to turn. I say, *Alleluia!* What better time to come into fullness in your relationship with God?

One thing is for sure: For some, the awareness of their brokenness and need for God's grace and forgiveness is very real in this place of exile. The pain is real and so is the hope.

Photo: Chris Tumilty

Compunction and Grace

Compunction is the realization that one has done something harmful to the human soul, something that propels us into despair, fearing that we may have crossed a line from which there is no return, and the deep knowing, even the agonizing awareness, of our need of grace. When we are met in this space by the awareness of God's forgiveness and love, we are brought back to our most authentic and sacred self. I have witnessed this amazing grace more in exile behind bars than anywhere else in my life, and it never ceases to floor me. I'm struck by the humility of the penitent human heart, by the stunning and loving grace of God and the pure sacredness of each moment. Yes, this is where we know that God is in full solidarity with us in our struggle and in our joy. This is where the brokenness of the human heart is held and healed by the balm of God's incredible love.

I could tell a thousand stories about grace and struggle and beauty in the jails, because each person is a story in this *culture of grace* that is life with the incarcerated people of God. Jail is a place where different people co-exist and cultures clash and integrate. It's a place that is divided and yet a place where mutuality exists. It's a place where the lines are clearly drawn and then breached by both sides. It is a place of segregation and isolation, of unity and solidarity. Here, the fundamental sin of racism is evident and yet there are displays of dignity and mutual respect that defy that ugly truth. It can be dark and dangerous, yet filled with the sunlight of the spirit. It's a life in paradox – a house divided, and yet one that is in its own way crying out for the unifying force of God's love. It's messy and real here. In this place there is no hiding from yourself.

Amidst the struggle and despair, there is also a deep yearning for God. I know that in any given moment on any given day, there is more of prayer happening inside the walls of this jail than most anywhere else I know of. The inmates gather for small group Bible studies, attend spiritual formation programs, engage in contemplative practices such as Centering Prayer, attend Sunday Eucharist and meet regularly with our chaplains for pastoral care and spiritual direction. In many ways, this is my parish. Surely it is a holy place, this culture of compunction and grace. This is a place where the awareness of one's need of God's grace is very real. It is also a place where the experience of God's grace is very real, and there are moments when that grace cuts through all of the complexities of life here and we are allowed to experience the breathtaking reality of God's grace and love up close.

✦   ✦   ✦

Grace

Black man wrapped in white.
he sits quietly reading
a tap on the glass
he turns toward the sound
with such grace
his smile welcomes the visitors
standing at his door
he sees friends
they see Jesus

the struggle of a lifetime
in the move from the bed to the chair
two more chairs please
for the friendly visitors

he says it for us
what we couldn't say
"I am dying
AIDS
" … it's ok."
such grace.

we talk
we pray
we find our dignity
through his.
he takes us to a place
I have never been
with his smile
with his tears
with his grace.

we thank God
we share bread.
with a touch
from a brother
the bishop anoints
and we remember
marked as Christ's own forever.
he falls into my arms
this angel with parched lips
and broken wings
such grace

—Brother Dennis

✦ ✦ ✦

Apple juice grace

One afternoon in our Sacred Journey Listening Circle we were sharing about moments of gratitude – talking about times when we felt close to God, and also about moments when things had been difficult. Damien began sharing about what it was like to be in the throes of kicking heroin addiction. The words falling from his trembling lips bore witness to the physical upheaval he was still experiencing, evident in his tense and nervous energy, in his desperate, fleeting eyes.

He described a moment when he was in IRC (Inmate Reception Center) being processed into the jail, which can sometimes take a few days. A nurse gave him a small container of apple juice to help calm the raging earthquake inside his body. He talked about how, even in that moment when the wildfire of addiction seemed insurmountable, he had never felt so grateful for a simple container of apple juice. He described how soothing it was as he felt the cool, sweet juice flow down his throat and into his stomach. Just speaking of the memory of that moment seemed to calm him as he sat in our circle.

Then, with our eyes fixed on one another, I said, "Sometimes God's grace comes in a carton of apple juice." The connection in the truth of this moment was also God's grace. Damien began to silently weep. It was as if something stuck within him had finally dislodged and thus opened a clearing space. No one said anything. We made room for the tears to flow and fall. Because sometimes our tears are our only words.

✦ ✦ ✦

All rise ...

As we held hands, the squeeze was so tight that it seemed like the bones might break. It had been four years, all of which Darryl and Dominique had spent locked up as the wheels of justice slowly turned. There had been two trials. The first ended in a hung jury. Now, after a second trial, we were at this moment. We had gotten the call early on a Friday morning that after two days of deliberations, the jury had reached a verdict. I rushed to the courthouse from the monastery in record time. I sat in the hallway with the family, feeling anxious, hopeful and powerless. The tension was thick. Small talk helped ease things. A burst of laughter broke through the tension; God's grace. It was a strange feeling, knowing that the verdict had been reached and some knew the fate of our friends, yet we didn't know. One thing we did know was that God was with us. Then the door opened and we were called in. The moment had come. At last.

I sat in the front row with Darryl's mom, Mary, our hands clasped and our hearts beating fierce with anticipation. Darryl and Dominique were brought in. They looked nervous yet calm and sharply focused. Darryl gave me a quick glance and a discreet nod. We had talked earlier during our allowed visit about holding fast to truth, faith and dignity. And there he sat, looking the world squarely in the eye.

The jury was brought in. Mary couldn't look at them. I did look at them, scanning for an indication, but there was nothing to read. Their steady gaze was fixed on the judge as he silently read the verdict. He handed the forms to the clerk and reminded us all that there was to be no emotional outburst when the verdicts were read.

All eyes were on the clerk as she began reading. After the required stating of case numbers and other details, the words came as we braced ourselves against each another. *"In the above entitled action, we the jury find the defendant ... NOT GUILTY."* The same verdict was repeated three more times – once for each charge per defendant. I was stunned by the words we were hearing. So many times, in many courtrooms, we have heard the worst. And even though I was convinced of Darryl and Dominique's innocence, I had braced myself for disappointment. Now, I heard gasps of whispered relief as if the weight of the world seemed to fall away. What we had always believed about Darryl and Dominique was confirmed by the jury. Mary was weeping into my chest. The attorneys were hugging their no-longer defendants after four years of struggle. Mary looked at the jury now with tears streaming down her face. I whispered to her, "Those people set your son free."

We were all stunned and relieved beyond belief. Mary said it over and over: "Thank you, God. Thank you, God." Then, in a moment I hope never to forget, I witnessed incredible grace as Dominique – sitting just a few feet in front of us, but still facing the front of the courtroom with her back to us – slowly bowed her head and raised her arms to the sky in reverence to God. Right there in the middle of it all, in the courtroom that had felt hostile to the truth for so long, where out of the dozen or so people involved in this trial – prosecutors, defense attorneys, court clerks, judge, bailiff, court stenographer – only the two defendants were black, truth and justice had finally prevailed. There was nothing left but to praise God.

We have dedicated our lives to walking the hard but grace-filled road with our incarcerated friends and this often means attending court appearances. It means a lot to see a friendly face in what can seem to be a hostile environment. I know; I've been there. For their families, it can be a fearful and confusing time.

We try to help them navigate the experience. Sometimes, just helping them understand the process – even though it might not be so good – can ease the anxiety because they have a sense of what to expect. Much of the time, we sit quietly in solidarity just doing our best to be a quiet, non-anxious presence.

✦ ✦ ✦

Cynthia's story is one of the most tragic I have ever heard. She was sexually assaulted for eight years by her stepfather and horribly abused by her mother her entire life. Despite all of her cries for help, no one came to her aid. The police ignored her cries; Child Protective Services ignored her cries. Then, at the age of fifteen, she fell into the hands of a controlling, abusive boyfriend, and what followed was the worst nightmare imaginable. Her boyfriend murdered her mother and stepfather. She was convicted as an accomplice even though she had no direct participation in those murders. She was tried as an adult, though she was just fifteen at the time. During her trial, her abuse, which had been reported to authorities on numerous occasions, was not allowed into evidence, the justification being that those events had no direct bearing on what happened the day of the murders. Cynthia's world was now collapsing, with her future in the hands of the system that had so dismally failed her all her life.

And then she met Sister Greta.

Greta's love and compassion became a lifeline and beacon of light and hope for Cynthia as the two walked the treacherous terrain together. Cynthia was transformed. Greta was transformed. We were all transformed. Through Greta's love, Cynthia was introduced to a real loving community for the first time in her life. We in turn were introduced to a beautiful young woman who inspires us all with her grace in the midst of darkness. At Cynthia's baptism at Los Padrinos Juvenile Hall, Sister Greta stood with her as her godmother. Cynthia had a real mother figure at last.

At Cynthia's sentencing, there was a moment that stunned the courtroom and held us all breathless. Sister Greta stood to address the court and talk, for the first time, directly and openly about all those who were supposed to protect Cynthia and had failed to do so. In a moment that is etched into my soul, Sister Greta then turned to Cynthia, in full view of those present that day and said, "Cynthia, we believe you and we believe in you. We will be with you every single day of the rest of your life, loving you. We are your family now. We will always be there for you."

Cynthia was sentenced to 51 years to life in prison.

Greta visits Cynthia and exchanges letters and phone calls regularly. Cynthia now has the motherly love and the family she has always desired and deserved and we have a beautiful young woman who inspires us all.

On Monday, October 1, 2018, Governor Jerry Brown signed into law the California State Senate Bill SB-1391, amending sentencing laws for fourteen and fifteen-year-olds. Cynthia will now be set free after being locked up for ten years.

✦ ✦ ✦

*No matter who you are, where you have been, what you
have done or had done to you,
no one is beyond the grace and love of God.*

—Brother Dennis

CHAPTER NINE

Seeing

Being seen is everything. For those who have been banished to the margins of our society, being seen feeds the
soul with dignity and a spirit of community. Mother
Teresa once said, "The most devastating form of hunger is that
of loneliness." I have also heard it said that the opposite of love is
not hate; it's indifference. I know these things are true because I
have lived them. To feel invisible brings deep sadness and affects
our sense of purpose and meaning of life. But to be seen can
revive our spirit. When I encounter brothers or sisters whose
only home is the streets, they may need a few bucks to get them
through, but what is also needed is a connection, a feeling that
they are part of the main stream of life. We all need to be reminded that we are part of the community. We all need to have
someone be curious about us and want to hear our story. When
we do that, we walk away feeling more connected to the real
community of all God's people.

Part of the covenant we make with God when being baptized

in the Episcopal Church is that we will proclaim the Good News of God in Christ, seek and serve Christ in all persons, loving our neighbors as ourselves, strive for justice and peace among all people and respect the dignity of every human being. All persons, all people and every human being means everybody. Period. No exceptions. These are pretty good principles to live by and ones that could, if taken seriously, have an enormous positive impact on the world and how each of us live, and move, and have our being with each other.

To strive for real justice, peace and respect for the dignity of every single person is vital to our identity, and the state of our criminal justice system and mass incarceration says a lot about who we are as a global community and society. But this problem of not seeing people isn't limited to the marginalized. How often do we really see the supermarket clerk, the parking garage attendant, the person taking tickets at the movies, or the person sitting across the dinner table?

In our Sacred Journey Listening Circles in the jails, some of the work we do together is a Seeing Practice, where we break into twos and the partners sit facing each other about three feet apart. The practice is to simply sit and connect with the other, to really see them, taking in everything about their face and energy. It is a profound practice, and one that can be uncomfortable at first, because we are not accustomed to connecting in that way. But when we stay with it, one thing that often comes out of that connection is a sense of compassion for the other.

Once, after a Sunday church service in jail, and we were saying our goodbyes, I looked at a friend who had shared his pain during the group reflection portion of the service. I said, "I see you." Tears welled up in his eyes. He hugged me. As we held each other, he whispered, "Thank you."

✦ ✦ ✦

In 2015 I traveled to Jeremie, Haiti, to visit the prison there. The conditions were horrible and inhumane. After entering through a steel security gate, one could see crude and suffocating concrete structures, with about twenty men crammed into each space approximately 30 feet square and only about six feet tall. There was no running water. No toilets. The only fresh air came from small openings in the wall facing where I was standing. I stood in the bright light of the sun, staring into the darkness of the cell. When the men saw me, some would appear from the blackness and move to the window. I don't speak Haitian Creole, but in preparation for the trip, I had made little slips of paper about the size of bookmarks. One side read "Mwen wè ou," which means "I see you." On the other side of the paper, it said, "Bondye wè ou," meaning "God sees you." This simple gesture made the connection, as several men motioned, pointing first to their eyes, then to me. They saw me. Once, I put my hand on my heart as I pointed to the word "Bondyè," God's love. A man reached through the open space, pulled my arm through it, and placed my hand on his heart. Then he reached through and placed his hand on my heart. It was one of the most powerful moments of human connection that I have ever experienced, and not a word was spoken except the language of the heart.

Never underestimate the power of being seen.

Two years later we traveled to the T. Don Hutto Detention Center in Texas for women immigrants with a contingent of other Episcopalians committed to criminal justice reform, to stand in solidarity with the women imprisoned there. Hundreds of us stood on the road facing the prison. Then I noticed that one of the women was moving something white up and down the thin slit of the vertical window – a white towel or piece of paper. I realized that the women were waving at us. I began waving back and shouting, "I see you!" Soon, all the others were waving and chanting "I see you!" "Te vio!" Later, we heard that the women contacted a representative of the Episcopal Church to say that all the time we were standing outside, they were huddled around the windows, and stayed there until the last of our group left. They wanted us to know that they saw us and it meant everything to them that we were there for them. There is no doubt that we were seen by God that day. It means everything to be seen, to know that you are not alone. The impact of being truly seen is of inestimable value to the human spirit. Seeing and being seen are essential to returning to our sacred self.

✦   ✦   ✦

Photo: Chris Tumilty

I met Daniel in the summer of 2016. He had been arrested and jailed on charges stemming from an incident at a Hollywood drug store. Daniel was trying to cash a check – a check that actually belonged to him. The known facts are that Daniel was unarmed, not breaking any laws or causing any disruptions. And he is black. Although he was confused as a result of an imbalance in his medication, the store security tape showed that he was calm and posing no threat to anyone. Nonetheless, the police were called. Within minutes of the two police officers arriving at the scene, a struggle ensued, and Daniel was shot three times. He was charged with two counts of attempted murder of police officers.

· I have been a chaplain in the L.A. County Jails for many years. I have seen a lot and I have met a lot of different types of people. I am not easily fooled. I know that many of our incarcerated friends would do well to admit culpability. I am not shy about the importance of that kind of accountability, and I try to guide them in that process. But that was not the nature of my relationship with Daniel. After our first meeting, I found myself wondering what a young man like him was doing in jail. Daniel is a good man. He is thoughtful, respectful, generous, patient, warm and kind. He is talented, bright and engaging. He truly is a man of peace who has brought light to the dark corners of the jail. Everyone could see it. I also saw in Daniel what I have seen in others over the years when they are unfairly trapped in our broken criminal justice system. It's grace. It's civility. And it is impressive.

There is no doubt in my mind that our world – including our criminal justice system – would be a better place if we could just see people for who they truly are – see the goodness of a person as our starting point when considering their circumstances, instead of being blinded by hasty and false conclusions. How different things might be if we just took the time to really see people, to see their inherent goodness instead of their fault lines. Every person is more – much more – than the worst thing they have done or had done to them. Daniel included.

+ + +

The Gospel according to Luke tells a story that illustrates the power of being seen.[1] In the story, a woman quietly moves through the crowd, unnoticed by most. She had been crippled for eighteen years. She enters a synagogue bent over, head down. It's not easy for her to make the trip, but there she is, to worship God. There is nothing in the text that indicates that she asks for anything – not mercy, not pity, not even healing. The woman is un-named in this account, which seems particularly telling. There is a moment embedded in this story that is important. It says that Jesus *saw her*. In the midst of the crowd and noise, Jesus turns his attention to this unassuming woman. He calls to her, and with his gentle eyes and worker's hands he reaches out ... with a word ... with a touch ... with love. And just like that, after eighteen years, she is healed. She looks into the eyes of Jesus and sees love. She looks into the eyes of the religious leaders and sees rage. I wonder if the leader of the synagogue was also bent over under the weight of his own short-sightedness and narrow-mindedness. We all need liberation – some from suffering and oppression, and others from privilege.

When we truly see each other, amazing things can happen. In that simple gesture, the weight of the world can be lifted, and together we can move from death to life. When we truly see one another and mirror our sacred self for each other, we just might catch a glimpse of heaven right here on earth.

---

1. Luke 13:10 – 17

CHAPTER TEN

Returning

I have learned that this spiritual journey we call life is about returning to our most authentic self, as God created us and desires us to be. It's about returning to our true core self.

At our monastery, we have a labyrinth, which is an ancient form of walking meditation. Anyone who has walked a labyrinth knows that at times it feels as if you are headed away from the center, but you never really are. If you just stay the course and trust the path, eventually you will arrive at the heart of the labyrinth.

My life has been like the labyrinth walk. There have been many switch-backs and changes in direction. Finding my way to the center will continue to be the work of a lifetime, but along the way I catch glimpses of it. With each step, I allow myself to spiral deeper into my sacred self and union with the divine, and I know that all of us can have that right here, right now.

Eternal life may indeed be "out there" somewhere, but it is also as close as our next heartbeat and our next breath. Jesus said the

Photo: Mitch Garcia

kingdom of heaven is not only around us, but within us.[2] This is
the narrow gate that leads to life – divine life – and it is there for
all of humanity. It spans the spectrum of religious and spiritual
experience of all human kind, never bound exclusively to any
one tradition or denomination. This is the Good News for all
people, and we can have it now, if we choose it for ourselves.

My friend and teacher James Finley tells a parable to illustrate
this truth. He asks us to imagine that we are sitting at a table with
God, and God says, "All your life we have done things on your
terms. But there will come a time when we will do it on mine,
and you don't have to wait until you die for that to happen."

I don't want to wait until I die to realize the fullness of life
that God desires for me. I want to experience the kingdom of
heaven within, right here and now, so I will keep putting one
foot in front of the other in this labyrinth walk of life, trusting
the path. Every once in a while, something will happen. In those

---

2. Luke 17:21

moments, I sense the nearness of my Creator, standing with me at the center of my life, and I catch a glimpse of heaven right here on earth.

✦ ✦ ✦

I spent much of my life lost, desperately running from how I felt about myself and running toward whatever I thought might fix me. No amount of booze, drugs, lovers, success or money could satisfy the longing within me. Modern western culture conditions us to think that material success and achievement will fix us. We think if we just have the right address, the right amount of money in the bank, the right partner on our arm, the right this or the right that, it will somehow fill the aching void within us. I thought, mistakenly, that these things would heal the wounds of shame, anger and sense of unworthiness. Maybe I even thought that they might prove to the world that I wasn't crazy after all, and also quiet that voice that said I would never amount to anything. The problem is that this mindset of material accumulation to fill the void works – for a long time, it worked for me – until it doesn't. These things only mask the problems and keep us from being honest enough to do the work that is necessary for healing and restoring our lives. We all have our wounds. We all have our own prisons.

The restorative work of healing our wounds and breaking down the walls of our personal prisons is the narrow gate that leads to life. It is found through the difficult work of getting honest with ourselves. I have found the fearless and searching inventory work of Twelve Step Spirituality to be an opening for the narrow gate. I have found it through understanding that in order to have true compassion for the world around me, I must first cultivate it for myself. I have also found it in the crucible times with my friends in jail. I have seen it in moments of compunction and grace flooding us with love when everything is stripped away but the truth of who we are: the absolute apple of God's eye and beloved, not in spite of our brokenness, but because of it.

Lazarus

I can relate to the story of Jesus raising Lazarus from the dead.[3] In it, Lazarus had been dead for three days, which tells me that he was really dead, no doubt about it. In order to achieve sobriety and freedom in recovery, I had to be free of any idea that I could continue on the way I was. The old, false self needed to die. I had to die in order to live.

It's a mysterious thing how Lazarus heard the voice of Jesus calling from the tomb of death. God reaches us in the darkness. It's the homing device that continues to pulse within us, calling us to our true home. There is a place deep within each of us that is the divine; this is where God resides within us and it is pure light. It is out of reach of the corruption of life, out of reach of even death. It's from this deeper place that we hear the beckoning of God, continually calling us to new life – the life that God desires for us, the life that returns us to our sacred self. Returning to this most authentic self requires that we work though the layers of our wounds that prevent us from living fully in freedom. We almost always need others to help us along this path of healing. I know I did.

When Lazarus stepped out of the tomb of death, his hands and head were bound in strips of cloth. Jesus then tells those

---

3. John 11:38-44

who were there to "Unbind him, and let him go." It was the community around Lazarus that removed the wrappings of death so that he could be set free. I think of this as being symbolic of all those things that bind us – all those false-self things like shame, arrogance, self-centeredness and addiction.

The list of our human frailties is long, and we need the help of a caring community around us to help free us. I tried doing things my way for a long time, and it drove me to the brink of insanity and death. Then I found a community of people who helped me recover from what Alcoholics Anonymous calls "the seemingly hopeless state of mind and body." I've had monks and the wider church community who have supported me in my spiritual life and faith. And surely I had – and still have – my dear friends living in exile in jails as companions along the way. All of us are teachers and students of one another on this amazing, sacred journey that has led us into the arms of God.

Life is lived in paradox. Suffering and grace live in mutuality. The Chinese philosophy of Yin and Yang says that all things exist as inseparable opposites. I cannot fully appreciate grace, joy, and light without the experience of struggle, sadness, and darkness. People who have experienced darkness and have found a way out, such as those who were once buried in addiction and made it through to a life of recovery, have an experiential understanding of death and resurrection. We know the Lazarus story because we have lived it. One can study about such things and gain an understanding, but to have lived the life is to come to a place of knowing. This is why the Lazarus story is important to so many who have come to know the truth for themselves about resurrection in this life – right here, right now.

✦ ✦ ✦

Most spiritual traditions teach a version of the Golden Rule – to treat others as you would like to be treated. Jesus teaches us to love our neighbor as ourselves. For half of my life, I didn't think much of myself. It was hard for me to consider that I loved myself because I had so many other programs of self-diminishment running in my head. So, for me, loving my neighbor as myself was a tricky proposition. In a way, I think we do love our neighbors as ourselves, and that's not always such good news. Personally, I carried so much shame and guilt and self-condemnation that at the least it prevented me from loving freely, and at the worst, I projected my sense of self onto those around me. If I couldn't see myself as beloved, how could I see others that way?

When I entered a life of recovery, I began – with the help of others – a real process of healing. It has included swallowing some hard truths about myself but also tending the delicate wounded places within me. It is an ongoing restorative process of healing that opens the space for compassion and self-love. It is only from this place that I can truly love my neighbor as myself in a healthy, life-giving way. I'm still a work in progress, but I'm headed in the right direction. Each day, I come closer to a fuller understanding of what it means for me to love God with everything I have and to love my neighbor as myself, knowing that the two are inextricably connected. We are all in union with God and one another. How I am in relationship with others is how I am in relationship with God. Slowly, day by day, I am beginning to know what it is to truly see myself and others as God see us.

✦ ✦ ✦

In 2016, I traveled to Nampa to visit my family. During that trip, I suggested that I would like to return to our father's grave.

I invited others to join me, not completely expecting anyone to take me up on the offer. But they did. My brother Bob and his wife Mary, my sister Peggy and her husband Bob and my younger brother Russ were all there. I rode out with my brother Bob, just like we did that day nearly twenty years earlier. We walked around the cemetery as we waited for the others to arrive. We talked about our lives. I told him that I respected him as the elder of the family now. Bob truly is a lot like our dad, and on that day, I embraced that and honored him for it. It was awkward for him to accept it, but I could feel it meant something to him. I think in that moment he felt seen. We talked about alcoholism. He said something about how much I had been through and how he admired my path. That day, it felt like we made a connection, as brothers, in a new way. It felt good.

When the others arrived, we all gathered around our dad's grave – the same place where Bob had watched me kneel down and kiss the frozen ground all those years ago. I started by telling a story about Dad taking me fishing when I was a boy. Others told stories about life with him. We laughed and we cried. We talked with him as if he were standing right there with us. It was if our father was holding us all in a way that we had not been able to hold one another before. It was beautiful.

That day at the grave was a resurrection moment for us. We confessed and forgave and loved each other. The road of returning us to one another was long, but we made it. We still disagree about some things, but we can all agree on the most important thing. We are family.

The glory of God is the human person fully alive.

—Irenaeus of Lyon

Is not salvation about fully becoming who we are created to be? And could it be that our true primary purpose in this life is to help one another discover – or rediscover – our most authentic self – our sacred self? If that sounds like lofty language, it should, because it is. There is nothing less than the Kingdom of Heaven at stake, and it's within each of us. Salvation of my soul isn't something outside myself to be achieved as some sort of reward for a successful endeavor. It is an experience within me, to be realized in every moment of every day. Because isn't today all we really have?

I appreciate the idea of *one day at a time* brought forth in the A.A. program. When I first came into recovery, the idea of staying sober for the rest of my life was unthinkable. I struggled to get even one hour of sobriety. But the idea of just one day at a time was something that worked for me. Each and every day in my life since has been a day of salvation. Jesus reinforces this idea when he says, "So do not worry about tomorrow, for tomorrow will bring worries of its own. Today's trouble is enough for today."[4] For me, salvation is an ongoing process of continuous spiritual experiences that have led to a larger spiritual awakening in my life. In short, salvation is found on the ground in the moment. This is most evident in moments of solidarity with friends in suffering and grace, when the reality of God's love is such that we connect with our truest self and embrace the beauty of being fully human. Salvation is about wholeness of life. It's about becoming everything God created us to be, and it's the work of a lifetime – one day, one breath, one heartbeat at a time. We don't have to look to somewhere beyond ourselves in the moment. The hope of salvation is within each moment of life.

---

4. Matthew 6:34

I have been fortunate to find my way to the monastery. Life here is intentionally focused on the pursuit of our most authentic and sacred self. Grounded in praying in community four times each day, our work around the monastery, study of holy scripture and other sacred texts and living a good deal of our time together in silence has undoubtedly taken me deeper into wholeness of life with God, myself and with others. When I step out of the enclosure and into the jails, it is a penitent walk. It is my *metanoia*, which means changing one's way of life as a result of penitence and spiritual conversion. The ministry in the jails is my source of salvation that brings me to wholeness of life, where I realize more and more each day my sacred self as God created me.

But one doesn't need to enter the monastic life to discover these truths. Wholeness of life is for everyone, everywhere. Your sacred self is waiting to be rediscovered, right where you are. God's desire – that divine ember within you – longs for you to simply fan the flame. But you must be bold and audacious. Bold like Jacob, who wrestled with the angel of God through the night and wouldn't let him go until he received God's blessing.[5] Audacious like the woman who pushed through the crowd and reached out to touch the hem of Jesus' robe, refusing to let the moment pass her by.[6] It requires that we never give up, that we are as relentless in our pursuit of God as God is relentless in love for us. It requires that we claim what we need from God and not settle for anything less.

My prayer is that each of us become who we are and always have been – our sacred-self that knows that we are worthy, that we are beloved by God, that we are the absolute apple of God's

---

5. Genesis 32:22-32
6. Mark 5:25-34

eye and that all of us are heirs – through hope – of God's ever-lasting kingdom.

Take the risk. Surrender to grace. And fall into the arms of our loving God.

> *"Come to the edge," he said.*
> *"We can't, we're afraid!" they said.*
> *"Come to the edge," he said.*
> *"We can't, we will fall!" they said.*
> *"Come to the edge," he said.*
> *And so they came.*
> *And he pushed them.*
> *And they flew.*
>
> —Guillaume Apollinaire (1880-1918)

◆ ◆ ◆

A Prayer for Aimee

Holy God, you brought your people out of slavery, sustained them in the wilderness, and delivered them into freedom. Reach my dear daughter Aimee. Unbind her from the chains of addiction and bring her safely back home.

Aimee, you have been lost for so long. But you are not as far away as it may seem. You are not beyond the grace and love of God. I pray for you each day. I pray that you will be able to make the turn – the simple decision to choose life in recovery. Come home, dear one, to the life that God intends for you. Come home. We are all waiting for your return. Like the father who watches for his prodigal child to appear on the horizon, I long for the day that I will run to you and celebrate life together in recovery.

I know that somewhere within, you hear our prayers for you. Like a homing device of love within your heart that continues to pulse even in the depths of the sea of despair, so our love beats for you.

Come back, my dear daughter Aimee, from the land of oblivion.

—Dennis Gibbs

Gratitude

There are many to thank for bringing this book forward and to whom I extend my heart in deepest gratitude. To Sister Greta Ronningen, my true spiritual sister and teacher, who encouraged me to be brave enough to speak my truth, and without whom this book would not exist. To Sharon Crandall, who reminds me daily that love is all there is. To Greg Boyle, for being a prophet of love and teacher of truth in our time. To Don Maxwell, who has walked the road of recovery with me for over two decades and taught me so much of what it means to be a man and what a father/son relationship can be. With deep appreciation for my family, especially my sweet sister, Peggy, who never gave up on me and is always there when it counts the most. You are a model of maternal love, so needed in our world today.

Thank you to my companions on the way in the Episcopal Church, especially Bishop John Harvey Taylor, who gave this project the go-ahead. To my parish, The Church of Our Saviour, San Gabriel, California, for its tremendous support over the years. To Bob Williams and Janet Kawamoto of Cathedral Center Press, who made it all happen. A special nod of respect and admiration to my editors, Lizze Slocum and Alysha Kawamoto, not only for making this a better book but for making me a better writer. Thanks to Chris Tumilty, photographer, for his talent in capturing life in the jails in such an intimate and honoring way, and to Carrie Voris, who captured my vision with her amazing graphic artist touch.

Great love goes out to my recovery community, who brought me in from the cold, dark night and taught me how to live as a sober man with purpose. To my monastic community, including our Oblates and Divine Companions, who have shown me what a real community built on love and desire for God can lead to. And to all of my brothers and sisters living in exile in jails and prisons – those I have met and not met along the way. You have inspired not only this book, but my life.

San Gabriel, California
February 2019

✦   ✦   ✦

 To learn more about the ministry of PRISM Restorative Justice in the Diocese of Los Angeles, visit the website at www.prismjustice.org.

To learn more about the Community of Divine Love monastery, visit www.cdlmonks.org.

38850771R00109

Made in the USA
Middletown, DE
13 March 2019